A Study on Form-meaning Relation from the Neuro-cognitive Perspective

Zhang Shiqian

AMERICAN ACADEMIC PRESS

This book is supported by the Humanities and Social Science Youth Foundation of the Ministry of Education of China (Grant Number: 22YJC740099)

本书为教育部人文社科青年基金项目（项目号：22YJC740099）成果

AMERICAN ACADEMIC PRESS

Published in the United States of America

By AMERICAN ACADEMIC PRESS

201 Main Street

Salt Lake City

UT 84111 USA

Email manu@AcademicPress.us

Visit us at http://www.AcademicPress.us

ISBN: 979-8-3370-8913-3

Word Count: 254,225

Distributed to the trade by National Book Network Suite 200, 4501 Forbes Boulevard, Lanham, MD 20706

10 9 8 7 6 5 4 3 2 1

Manufactured in the United States of America

Preface

The most fundamental issue in linguistic theory is the nature of meaning and how to deal with it (Jackondoff, 1990, 2002, 2007). The form-meaning relation, i.e., the semiotic embodiment relation between linguistic expression (structure) and meaning, is one of the focuses of contemporary linguistic research. Early linguistic studies in this field mainly concentrate on the precise description of the form-meaning relation. However, language is one part of the brain cognition, so the semiotic embodiment relation between linguistic expression and meaning must have its neuro-cognitive basis and does not violate the feasibility of neural operation. (Lamb, 1966, 1999; Cheng, 2002, 2005, 2006)

Many theoretical approaches have been applied to the research of form-meaning relations. For instance, the formal semanticists (e.g., Maria Aloni, Paul Dekker, & Floris Roelofsen, 2016), the Case Grammar (Fillmore, 1968, 1982, 1997), the Lexical Semantics (Levin, 1993, Levin & Rappaport Hovav, 1998, 1999, 2005), and the Construction Grammar (Goldberg, 1995) took certain factors, such as the (logical) truth value, the semantic role, the lexical semantics, and the syntactic structure as the determinants of form-meaning relation; but they neglected the "meaning" in the brain, (i.e., the concepts in the mind). Conceptual meaning is a main concern of Cognitive Linguists.

Cognitive Linguistics is an approach of language research that focuses on human experiences and the way we perceive and conceptualize the world, which suggests that language is one part of human cognition and linguistic investigation contributes to the understanding of human mind (Cheng, 2002). A lot of cognitive linguistic theories concerned about the conceptual meaning in the brain that based on human experiences, however, none of them has payed special attention to the sensory-motor practices, which is the physical bases of human experiences and the sources of the "meaning" in the mind.

Cheng (2002, 2005, 2006) proposed the Cognitive-Functional Approach of linguistic study, which focuses mainly on the relationship between the conceptual meaning and the syntactic expression as well as the mental operation of linguistic system. According to this approach, there exist a connection between the perceptual-locomotor system and the linguistic expression system, with the joint between them being the conceptual meaning system (Cheng, 2002, 2005, 2006); the conceptual meaning forms with the grammatical structure a representative relation through grammatical meaning (Cheng 2006: 71), in which way the form-meaning relation is turned into the relation between the form (grammatical structure) and

I

the brain (conceptual meaning). This approach constructed the "Conceptual Frame" (Cheng, 2002, 2005, 2006), later developed into the "Cognitive Event Frame" (Cheng, 2019, 2020), to "formally represent the conceptual content of clauses", which are effective tools of formulating conceptual contents. Although this approach payed attention to the connection between the sensory-motor system, the linguistic expression system, and the conceptual meaning system, its theoretical framework is still a form-brain two level framework. Cheng (2019, 2020) points out that this theoretical approach still needs verification by analyzing various cognitive events and their constructions.

The perspective of the Embodied Cognition, which is a new research approach of cognitive science proposed on the bases of abundant neuro-cognitive evidence, suggests that "cognition is a kind of highly embodied, scenario-based activities; it is also a kind of experiences depending on certain prototypes and generated from the interaction between one's body and its environment" (Anderson, 2003). The perspective of the Embodied Language of Cognition suggests that language roots in the human sensory-motor system, emphasizing the function of experiences (Glenberg, 1997; Barsalou, 1999); it is further proposed that language processing are the mental simulation processes of the operation of the sensory-motor system and related experiences (Guan, 2007).

Under the perspective of the Embodied Language of Cognition (Glenberg, 1997; Barsalou, 1999; Anderson, 2003), this book proposes a theoretical framework (hypothesis): the form-meaning relation in language shall be a three-dimensional interactive relation between body (the sensory-motor system) — brain (the mental network of the experiential knowledge) — form (the language expression system), rather than be a two dimensional relation between meaning and form. Body is the original source of "meaning". The specific "meaning" comes from the body (the sensory-motor practices), (which become a part of the experiential knowledge network) stored in the brain and embodied as certain language form (expression); at the same time, the processing of certain language expression needs to extract the "meaning" (related experiential knowledge) from the brain, which in turn actives the "meaning" (related sensory-motor experiences) from the body. The brain is the core of the three-dimensional interactive relation, which joints the body and the language expression.

There are some events, such as the obtaining event, the physical contact event, the delivery event, and the throwing event, that are parts of human daily activities. Different actions/practices belonging to one type of event would be processed, integrated, and stored in the brain to form the experiential knowledge network of this type of event and be construed as different verbs and constructions of this type of event in language usage. These events and their language expressions (i.e., verbs and constructions) are typical materials to test the neural feasibility and descriptive effectiveness of linguistic approaches.

As a consequence, the main objective of the present book is to test the feasibility of the "body—brain—form" theoretical framework (hypothesis), i.e., to test whether it can effectively explain the cognitive operation and the usage-distribution of the language system. To address this issue, this book takes certain daily event, i.e., the obtaining event, as an example to explain the interaction between its sensory-motor practices, its brain experiential knowledge network, and the construal of its (English) constructions. Beside, this book would adopt the "Cognitive Event Frame" (Cheng, 2019, 2020) to formulate the brain experiential knowledge network (the conceptual content) of the obtaining event, which is an effective and economical tool in formulating conceptual contents. Moreover, this book would build corpuses of different types of obtaining verbs and constructions, and use quantitative analysis to test the effectiveness and accuracy of the "body—brain—form" approach in explaining the neural operation and the usage-distribution of the language system.

Besides the main objective, this book also reports several data analysis cases under the framework of the "Conceptual Frame" approach (Cheng, 2002, 2005, 2006) to further verify the effectiveness of this approach in formulating conceptual contents, including the analysis on the physical contact event and its (English) constructions and the comparative analysis on the throwing event and its Chinese and English constructions and that on the delivery event and its Chinese and English constructions.

Contents

Chapter One Introduction

————————◆ ◆━◆·◆¼◆·◆━◆ ◆————————

1.1 Background of the Research

The most fundamental issue in linguistic theory is the nature of meaning and how to deal with it (Jackondoff, 1990, 2002, 2007). The form-meaning relation, i.e., the semiotic embodiment relation between linguistic expression (structure) and meaning, is one of the focuses of contemporary linguistic (theoretical) research. Early linguistic studies in this field mainly concentrate on the precise description of the form-meaning relation. However, language is one part of the brain cognition, so the semiotic embodiment relation between linguistic expression and meaning must have its neuro-cognitive basis and does not violate the feasibility of neural operation. (Lamb, 1966, 1999; Cheng, 2002, 2005, 2006)

Many theoretical approaches and descriptive methodologies have been applied to the research of form-meaning relations. The formal semanticists (e.g., Maria Aloni, Paul Dekker, & Floris Roelofsen, 2016) employ truth value to deal with the relation between the connotation of a clause and the lexical meaning. Case Grammar by Fillmore (1968, 1982, 1997) suggests that each semantic role defines a natural class of arguments, with members of this natural class usually having a common semantic relation to certain types of verbs as well as some shared options for their morpho-syntactic expression. Levin's Lexical Semantics holds that verbs can be classified according to the language structures they distribute, and syntactic structures are projected from verb's lexical meaning, that is, lexical semantics determines syntactic structures in language (Levin, 1993, Levin & Rappaport Hovav, 1998, 1999, 2005). Construction Grammar (Goldberg, 1995) attributes the differences of the verb meanings in different constructions (syntactic structures) directly to the constructions. It claims that the core meaning of a verb fuses with the event meanings represented by syntactic constructions or associates with particular syntactic positions of certain substructures. These approaches explain the form-meaning relation from different perspectives, however, none of them has consider the conceptual meaning (conception in the mind) in discussing form-meaning relations, which is the main concern of Cognitive Linguists.

Cognitive Linguistics is an approach of language research that focuses on human experiences and the way we perceive and conceptualize the world, which suggests that language is one part of human cognition and linguistic investigation contributes to the understanding of human mind (Cheng, 2002). In contrast to the viewpoint that linguistic ability is dependent on other basic cognitive systems and abilities, such as perception, memory, and categorization, Cognitive Linguistics emphasizes the indistinction between language and other intellectual abilities and language is viewed as an integral facet of cognition rather than a distinct, self-contained system (as a separate "module" or "mental faculty") (Shu, 2008). Many theories of Cognitive Linguistics, such as Semantic Structure (Jackondoff, 1990, 2002, 2007), Cognitive Semantics (Talmy, 1991; 2000a; 2000b), Construction Grammar (Goldberg, 1995, 2010), Cognitive Grammar (Langacker, 1987, 1990, 1991), have had the idea of analyzing language by connecting to the functions of brain cognition. A lot of cognitive linguistic theories concerned about the conceptual meaning in the brain that based on human experiences, however, none of them has payed special attention to the sensory-motor practices, which is the physical bases of human experiences and the sources of "meaning" in the mind.

Absorbing the ideas of some approaches of Cognitive Linguistics (e.g., Talmy, 1991, 2000a, 2000b; Langacker, 1987, 1990, 1991), Neurocognitive Linguistics (Lamb, 1966, 1999) and the Systematic Functional Grammar (Halliday, 1994), Cheng (2002, 2005, 2006) proposed the Cognitive-Functional Approach of linguistic study, which focuses mainly on the relationship between the conceptual meaning and the syntactic expression as well as the mental operation of linguistic system. This approach emphasizes the experiential knowledge stored in the brain and the inseparability of the encyclopedia knowledge with the lexical meaning of verbs (Cheng 2006:48). According to this approach, there exist a connection between the perceptual-locomotor system and the linguistic expression system, with the joint between them being the conceptual meaning system (Cheng, 2002, 2005, 2006); the conceptual meaning forms with the grammatical structure a representative relation through grammatical meaning (Cheng 2006: 71), in which way, the form-meaning relation is turned into the relation between form (grammatical structure) and the brain (conceptual meaning). This approach constructed the "Conceptual Frame" (Cheng, 2002, 2005, 2006), later developed into the "Cognitive Event Frame" (Cheng, 2019, 2020), to "formally represent the conceptual content of clauses", which are quite effective tools of formulating conceptual contents. Although this approach payed attention to the connection between the sensory-motor system, the linguistic expression system, and the conceptual meaning system, its theoretical framework is still a form-brain two level framework.

The perspective of the Embodied Cognition, which is a new research approach of cognitive science proposed on the bases of abundant neuro-cognitive evidence (e.g., Tettamanti et al, 2005; Zwaan, 2006; Whiteny, 2009), suggests that "cognition is a kind of highly embodied, scenario-based activities; it is also a kind of experiences depending on certain prototypes and generated from the interaction between one's body and its environment" (Anderson, 2003). The perspective of the Embodied Language of Cognition suggests that language roots in the human sensory-motor system, emphasizing the function of experiences (Glenberg, 1997; Barsalou, 1999); it is further proposed that language processing are the mental simulation processes of the operation of the sensory-motor system and related experiences (Guan, 2007).

1.2 Objective of The Research

Under the perspective of the Embodied Language of Cognition (Glenberg, 1997; Barsalou, 1999; Anderson, 2003), this book proposes a theoretical hypothesis: the form-meaning relation in language shall be a three-dimensional interactive relation between body (the sensory-motor system) — brain (the mental network of the experiential knowledge) — form (the language expression system), rather than be a two dimensional relation between meaning and form. The specific "meaning" comes from the body (the sensory-motor practices), (which become a part of the experiential knowledge) stored in the brain, and embodied as certain language form (expression); at the same time, the processing of certain language expression needs to extract the "meaning" (related experiential knowledge) from the brain, which in turn actives the "meaning" (related sensory-motor experiences) from the body. The brain is the core of the three-dimensional interactive relation, which connects the body and the language expression.

The theoretical hypothesis of the "body—brain—form" three-dimensional relation has not been systematically studied and tested. Cognitive linguistics focuses on language usage (Lamb, 1966, 1999). Since the core of the "body—brain—form" three-dimensional relation is the brain, to test the feasibility of this approach, we shall consider whether it can theoretically describe the experiential knowledge network (i.e., the conceptual content) in the brain, and whether it can effectively explain the cognitive operation as well as the usage-distribution of the language system.

According to the Cognitive-Functional Approach (Cheng, 2002, 2005, 2006), conceptual meaning forms with grammatical structure representational relation through grammatical meaning (Cheng 2006: 71), consequently, the form-meaning relation is turned into the relation between form (grammatical structure) and brain (conceptual meaning). Although this approach did not directly include the level of body (the sensory-motor system) in its form-brain theoretical framework, it has paid attention to the connection between the three, which is in line with the viewpoint of the Embodied Language of Cognition (Glenberg, 1997; Barsalou, 1999; Anderson, 2003). Cheng (2002, 2005, 2006) constructed the "Conceptual Frame" to "formally represent the conceptual content of clauses", which forms with the grammatical structure embodiment relation. This mechanism was later developed into the "Cognitive

Event Frame" (Cheng, 2019, 2020), which could both generally formulate the core conceptual content of an event and subtly formulate the elaborated conceptual contents of different actions of a type of event. Both frames are quite effective and economical tools in formulating the conceptual contents of clauses/events. Cheng (2019, 2020) points out that this theoretical approach still needs verification by analyzing various cognitive events and their constructions.

There are some events, such as the physical contact event, the delivery event, the throwing event, and the obtaining event, that are parts of human daily activities. Different actions/practices belonging to one type of event would be processed, integrated, and stored in the brain to form the experiential knowledge network of this type of event and be construed as different verbs and constructions of this type of event in language usage. These events and their language expressions (i.e., verbs and constructions) are typical materials to test the neural feasibility and descriptive effectiveness of linguistic theories.

The main objective of the present book is to test the feasibility of the "body—brain—form" theoretical framework (hypothesis), i.e., to test whether it can effectively explain the cognitive operation and the usage-distribution of the language system. To address this issue, this book takes certain daily event, i.e., the obtaining event, as an example to explain the interaction between its sensory-motor practices, its brain experiential knowledge network, and the construal of its (English) constructions. Beside, this book would adopt the "Cognitive Event Frame" (Cheng, 2019, 2020) to formulate the brain experiential knowledge network (the conceptual content) of the obtaining event, which is an effective and economical tool in formulating conceptual contents. Moreover, this book would build corpuses of different types of obtaining verbs and constructions, and use quantitative analysis to test the effectiveness and accuracy of the "body—brain—form" approach in explaining the neural operation and the usage-distribution of the language system.

Besides the main objective, this book also reports several data analysis cases under the framework of the "Conceptual Frame" approach (Cheng, 2002, 2005, 2006) to further verify the effectiveness of this approach in formulating conceptual contents, including the analysis on the physical contact event and its (English) constructions and the comparative analysis on the throwing event and its Chinese and English constructions and that on the delivery event and its Chinese and English constructions.

1.3 Methodology of The Research

The research of this book adopts a theory-data double driven method. The results of data analysis and quantitative analysis would be used to test theoretical hypothesis and support theoretical discussion; at the same time, existing theoretical perspective (i.e., the Embodied Language of Cognition) and hypothesis (i.e., the "body—brain—form" three-dimensional approach) would be adopted to guild the fixation of research aims, the design of the research, and the explanation of the results. Generally speaking, this book adopts a theory guiding empirical research and empirical data testing theory double driven methodology.

The following steps would be taken to build corpuses of different types of verbs and their constructions, based on which quantitative analysis would be done to test the effectiveness of the "body—brain—form" three-dimensional approach in explaining the neural operation and the usage-distribution of the language system. Step 1: To exhaustively collect English and Chinese verbs belonging to one type of event. English verbs would mainly be collected from Levin (1993)'s book: *English Verb Classes and Alternation*. Since the present book has different theoretical hypothesis from Levin (1993) concerning the form-meaning relation, the classes of verbs collected by the present book does not strictly follow their original category in Levin (1993)'s book. Then, according to the *Oxford Advanced Learner's English-Chinese Dictionary* (the 7th edition, 2009) and the *Contemporary Chinese Dictionary* (《现代汉语词典》, the 7th edition, 2016), the English verbs are translated into their Chinese correspondence. One English verb may correspond to more than one Chinese verbs according their meanings. Step 2: To consult authoritative English and Chinese dictionaries, for example, *A Dictionary of Current English Usage* (《现代英语用法词典》, Zhang, 2003), *A Dictionary of Chinese Verb Usage* (《汉语动词用法词典》, Meng, 1999), *Oxford Advanced Learner's English-Chinese Dictionary* (the 7th edition, 2009) and the *Contemporary Chinese Dictionary* (《现代汉语词典》, the 7th edition, 2016); corpuses, such as the COCA: Corpus of Contemporary American English (https://www.english-corpora.org/coca/), the BCC: BLCU Corpus Center (https://bcc.blcu.edu.cn/lang/zh) and the BNC: British National Corpus: (http://www.natcorp.ox.ac.uk/); and websites (e.g., Google, Baidu) to collect the usages and constructions of each selected verb. Step 3: To make a list of all the constructions that this kind of verbs could distribute. Step 4: Repeat Step 2 according to the construction list in Step 3, and to exhaustively complete the construction-list for each selected verb. If necessary, certain constructions may be made for a verb and be searched in these dictionaries, corpuses, and websites. Through this step, if certain constructions still cannot be supplemented for a verb, this verb would not be regarded to distribute in these constructions; if new constructions are found for this type of event, they would be supplemented into the list and for each verb. Step 5: After these steps, it could be regarded that the corpus has exhausted this type of verbs and their constructions to some extent, then the Statistical Table of Constructions of this type of event would be build, based on which quantitative analysis, such as the distribution frequency of this type of verbs in each construction and the usage frequency of each construction, could be made.

1.4 Outline of This Book

Chapter one is a brief introduction to the background, the objective, and the methodology of this book.

Chapter two is literature review. The research perspective of the Cognitive Linguistics (Jackendoff, 1990, 2002, 2007; Talmy, 1991; 2000a; 2000b; Goldberg, 1995; Longaker, 1987, 1990, 1991) is reviewed; then the study of (English) verbs under the Lexical Semantics (Levin, 1993) and that under the Construction Grammar (Goldberg, 1995) are reviewed; next, the Cognitive-Functional Approach (Cheng, 2002, 2005, 2006, 2019, 2020), its formulation tools (of conceptual content), i.e., the conceptual frame and the cognitive event frame, as well as its advantage and disadvantage are reviewed.

Chapter three introduced the theoretical hypothesis concerning the "Body—Brain—Form" three-dimensional interactive approach of form-meaning research.

Chapter four build corpus of the obtaining verbs and constructions, on the base of which quantitative analysis was conducted, and adopted the "Body—Brain—Form" approach to explain the interactive relation between the obtaining sensory-motor practices (i.e., the body), the mental network of the obtaining experiential knowledge (i.e., the brain), and specific obtaining verbs and constructions (i.e., the language form) to test the effectiveness and accuracy of the "body—brain—form" approach in explaining the neural operation and the usage-distribution of the language system. Besides, this chapter used the Cognitive Event Frame (Cheng, 2019, 2020) to formulate the core conceptual content and the elaborated conceptual content of the obtaining event to further verify the Cognitive Event Frame approach and add analysis case to it. The analysis of this section is based on the study of Zhang & Wang (2023).

Chapter Five, Six, and Seven reports several data analysis cases under the framework of the Conceptual Frame approach (Cheng, 2002, 2005, 2006) to further verify the effectiveness of this approach in formulating conceptual contents, including the analysis on the physical contact event and its (English) constructions and the comparative analysis on the throwing event and its Chinese and English constructions and that on the delivery event and its Chinese and English constructions. The analyses in these sections are based on the preliminary works done by Zhang Shiqian, Wangjia, and Lu Shengjin (e.g., Cheng & Zhang, 2012; Zhang & Wang, 2020).

Chapter Eight is a conclusion to the present book.

Chapter Two Literature Review

Cognitive Linguistics focuses on human experiences and takes conceptual meaning (conception in the brain, based on experiences) into consideration in explaining form-meaning relation (Cheng, 2002), which perspective is partially consistent with the present "body—brain—form" three-dimensional relation hypothesis. But cognitive linguistic approaches, including the Construction Grammar (Goldberg, 1995) and the Cognitive Event Frame approach (Cheng, 2002, 2005, 2006, 2019, 2020), have not taken the sensory-motor aspect, which is the basis of human experiences, into their theoretical system. Among the studies of form-meaning relation, three approaches, i.e., the Lexical Semantics (Levin, 1993), the Construction Grammar (Goldberg, 1995), and the Cognitive-Functional Approach (Cheng, 2002, 2005, 2006, 2019, 2020), are closely related with the research of the present book. Therefore, this book would mainly review these theories/approaches and compare them with the present "body—brain—form" three-dimensional relation hypothesis with respect to their effectiveness in explaining the neural operation and the usage-distribution of the language system.

2.1 Cognitive Linguistics

Cognitive Linguistics is an approach of language research that focuses on human experiences and the way we perceive and conceptualize the world, which suggests that language is one part of human cognition and linguistic investigation contributes to the understanding of human mind (Cheng, 2002). In contrast to the viewpoint that linguistic ability is dependent on other basic cognitive systems and abilities, such as perception, memory, and categorization, Cognitive Linguistics emphasizes the indistinction between language and other intellectual abilities, which view language as an integral facet of cognition rather than a distinct, self-contained system (as a separate "module" or "mental faculty") (Shu, 2008).

The common characteristics (viewpoints) of cognitive linguistic approaches include: (a) syntax is not autonomous, but it is a restrictive semiotic system of meaning expression; (b) meaning is conceptualization---the expressed meaning is the conception in human mind, and meaning is the relation between expression and mind; (c) semantics is "encyclopedic" but not "lexicographic", and various linguistic expressions are the point-cuts of an open knowledge network; (d) category has its organizational structure, which does not consist of a set of sufficient and necessary properties but is concerned with "typicality" and "similarity"; (e) grammaticality is vague, but not discrete; (f) there is resemblance between language ability and cognitive ability. In these six characteristics, the first five ones are concerned with conceptual meaning, which is a powerful notion introduced by cognitive linguists to the study of form-meaning relation. (Wilson & Keil, 1999:153)

In contrast with the viewpoints and research methods of traditional linguistics, especially the Transformational-Generative Grammar (Chomsky, 1981, 1982, 2000), the opinions hold by cognitive linguists about the essence of grammar and meaning are: (a) language system is not self-sufficient. Language knowledge is similar to the conceptual knowledge in other forms and its operational procedure is not substantively different from other cognitive abilities; (b) the grammatical structure, which serves as the construction of conceptual content and the symbolization of the restrictions, is not a self-sufficient formal system, but is symbolistic in nature. (c) the categories and structures in semantics, syntax, morphology and phonology are all abstracted from specific discourses, and the analysis of grammatical units must consult their semantic values. (Shu, 2008:16)

Many theories of Cognitive Linguistics, such as Semantic Structure (Jackendoff, 1990, 2002, 2007), Cognitive Semantics (Talmy, 1991; 2000a; 2000b), Construction Grammar (Goldberg, 1995), Cognitive Grammar (Langacker, 1987, 1990, 1991), and Metaphor Theory (Lakoff, 1987, 2014), have had the idea of analyzing language by connecting to the functions of brain cognition. These theories concerned about the conceptual meaning in the brain that based on human experiences, however, none of them pay attention to the sensory-motor system, which is the basis of human experiences.

2.2 Lexical Semantics

2.2.1 Levin's Lexical Semantics

The different classes of English verbs analyzed by this book would mainly be collected from Levin (1993)'s book: *English Verb Classes and Alternation*. Levin (1993) made a classification of different categories of English verbs from a lexical-semantic perspective and roughly described the relation between verbs and their variants. Since the present book has different theoretical hypothesis from Levin (1993) concerning the form-meaning relation, the classes of verbs collected by the present book does not strictly follow their original category in Levin (1993)'s book, that is, the present book may collect and reclassify English verbs according to the "body—brain—form" three-dimension interactive relation.

Levin's Lexical Semantics is guided by the assumption that the syntactic behavior of a verb, particularly with respect to the expression and interpretation of its arguments, is to a large extent determined by its meaning. Thus verb behavior can be used to predict the linguistically relevant aspect of verb meaning. (Levin, 1993, Levin & Rappaport Hovav, 1998, 1999, 2005)

In her book *English Verb Classes and Alternations* (1993)*,* Levin attempts to delimit and systematize verb behavior. Here, Levin's term of "alternation" has similar meaning with "construction" in the present book. She holds that, ideally, such a theory must provide linguistically motivated lexical entries for verbs which incorporate a representation of verb meaning and which allow the meanings of verbs to be properly associated with the syntactic expressions of their arguments. Levin suggests that the meaning of a verb can be the key to know its behavior. Presumably, predications about verb behavior are feasible because particular syntactic properties are associated with verbs of a certain semantic type.

Further examination of the nature of lexical knowledge confirms that various aspects of syntactic behavior of verbs are tied to their meanings. Moreover, verbs that fall into the same class according to shared behavior are expected to show shared meaning components. This point is demonstrated by extensive investigations of verbs: *break, cut, hit* and *touch*, including the research by Fillmore (1968, 1982, 1997) and that by Hale & Keyser (1999). These verbs differ with respect to their participation in diathesis alternations, as summarized in the table:

	touch	*hit*	*cut*	*break*
Conative	no	yes	yes	no
Body-part possessor ascension	yes	yes	yes	no
Middle	no	no	yes	yes

These studies suggest that the differences in verb behavior can be explained if the diathesis alternations are sensitive to particular components of verb meaning. For example, *touch* is a pure verb of contact; *hit* is a verb of contact by motion; *cut* is a verb of causing a change of state by moving something into contact with the entity that changes state, and *break* is a pure verb of change of state. The notions of motion, contact, change of state and causation that figure in these characterizations must be taken into account in selecting a lexical representation of verb meaning. These same notions are correlated with participation in diathesis alternations. (Levin 1993:1-10)

However, to determine the appropriate meaning components is not an easy task, since verbs can be classified according to different aspects of their meanings. What components of verb meaning figure in the predication of class membership and how does it project into the syntactic structure? Levin turns to event structure.

Early discussions hold that event structure representations typically involve two types of basic building block: 1) the "primitive predicates" that define the space of possible event structures; 2) the "idiosyncratic" element of verb's meaning which is called "constant" in early work since it is represented by a constant in a predicate decomposition (Levin & Hovav, 1991, 1995, 1998), and the accepted term is now "root". Besides, a stock of "event structure templates" is set for the various combinations of primitive predicates. They call the paring of a constant and an event structure template an event structure.

A root's most important property is its ontological type. There is a small set of these types, which include state, stuff, thing, place, manner and instrument. A root's ontological type largely determines its basic association with an event structure type. These associations can be expressed using "canonical realization rules" (Rappaport Hovav and B. Levin 1998, 2001), such as:

a. *dry* (externally caused state)→[[x ACT] CAUSE [y BECOME <DRY>]]

b. *bottle* (place) →[[x ACT] CAUSE [y BECOME IN <BOTTLE>]]

In the event structure the template is on the right of the arrows, the ontological type of the associated root is indicated in angle brackets; it is filled by the actual root when these templates are instantiated for particular verbs.

Then in which way is Event Structure approach superior to the representation of verb meaning based on semantic roles? It is easier to delimit a small set of grammatically relevant primitive predicates than it is to delimit a small set of grammatically relevant semantic roles. Indeed, relatively small sets of overlapping primitive predicates recur in various proposed systems of predicate decomposition, and the number of predicates is smaller than that of semantic roles (Levin & Rappaport Hovav, 1998, 1999, 2005).

But there are still problems in Event Structure approach. There are much more proposed sets of primitive predicates than typically acknowledged. Jackondoff (1990, 2002, 2007) augments many of the predicates with diacritics. But once predicates begin to proliferate, this theory encounters the same problems as theories of semantic roles: identifying a small, well-motivated set of primitive elements. What's more, most roots have a single ontological type, though some may have more than one. The latter can be matched with several event structure templates, leading to different verb senses. The classification of verbs by Levin's lexical semantic approach also has some problems which would be discussed in 2.2.3.

In conclusion, the main tenet of the Lexical Semantic Approach is that a verb has a structured lexical entry which alone determines the projection of its arguments (Chomsky 1981, 1986, 2000; Levin &

Pappaport Hovav 1995, 1998, 2005; Pinker 1989). Following this model, verbs with multiple meanings must have multiple lexical semantic representations, one for each meaning. These meanings, in turn, determine the various syntactic structures in which the verb can be distributed. In other words, argument alternations can be seen as a by-product of verbal polysemy (Levin & Pappaport Hovav, 2005). As a consequence, given the pervasiveness of verbal polysemy, the projectionist approach results in a significant proliferation of lexical representations associated with individual verbs.

2.2.2 Levin's Analysis and Classification of Verbs

The present book would take the physical contact verbs as examples to test the effectiveness of Levin's Lexical Semantics (1993) in classifying English verbs and in analyzing the relation between verbs and their constructions.

Based on the assumption that syntactic behavior of a verb, particularly with respect to the expression and interpretation of its arguments, is to a large extent determined by its meaning and that if the class members share certain meaning components they can be expected to exhibit the same syntactic behavior, Levin made classification of physical contact verbs in terms of their syntactic behavior.

According to Levin's analysis, the 18th class of verbs: Verbs of Contact by Impact can enter the following alternations (Levin, 1993: 148-153):

(1) With/Against alternation:

a. *Paula hit the stick against/on the fence.*

   (Doesn't imply: Paula hit the stick.)

b. *Paula hit the fence with the stick.*

   (Implies: Paula hit the fence.)

(2) Through/ With alternation:

a. **Paula hit the stick through/into the fence.*

b. *Paula hit the fence with the stick.*

(3) Conative alternation:

a. *Paula hit the fence (with the stick).*

b. *Paula hit at the fence (with the stick).*

(4) Body-part possessor ascension alternation:

a. *Paula hit Deirdre on the back.*

b. *Paula hit Deirdre's back.*

(5) Together reciprocal alternation (transitive):

a. *Paula hit one stick against another.*

b. *Paula hit the sticks together.*

(6) Simple reciprocal alternation (transitive):

a. *Paula hit one stick against another.*

b. **Paula hit the sticks.*

   (on the relevant reciprocal interpretration)

(7) *Causative alternations:

a. *Paula hit the fence (with a stick).*

b. **The fence hit with a stick.*

(8) *Middle alternation:

a. *Paula hit the fence.*

b. *The fence hit easily.*

(9) Instrument subject alternation:

a. *Paula hit the fence with the stick.*

b. *The stick hit the fence.*

(10) Unintentional interpretation available (some verbs):

a. Reflexive Object:

   Paula hit herself on the doorknob.

b. Body-Part Objective:

   Paula hit her elbow on the doorknob.

(11) Resultative phrase:

a. *Paula hit/kicked the door open.*

b. *Paula banged the window shut.*

The Hit verbs of 18.1, Swat verbs of 18.2, and Spank verbs of 18.3 share the meaning of moving one entity in order to bring it into contact with another entity, but they do not necessarily entail that this contact has any effect on the second entity.

One hallmark of Hit verbs is the with/against alternation. The Swat verbs do not show the with/against alternation. These verbs are found in the 'NP V NP with NP' frame, but not found in 'NP V NP against NP' frame. They do not allow instrument subjects. The Spank verbs are set apart because many of them are zero-related to nouns that refer to instruments used for hitting. They also do not allow instrument subjects. The Non-agentive Verbs of Contact by Impact describe instances of non-agentive contact by physical contact. They are used intransitively, as the complement of propositional phrase headed by *against*, a frame that could be viewed as the intransitive counterpart of the 'NP V NP against NP' frame associated with the Hit verbs

The 19th class: Poke verbs can enter *the with/against alternation, the through/with alternation, the conative alternation, the body-part possessor ascension alternation, *the causative alternation, and the instrument subject alternation. The Poke verbs describe bringing a pointed object into contact with a surface and, in some instances, puncturing the surface. The through/with alternation is characteristic of the verbs in this class. The 20th class: Verbs of Contact: Touch Verbs can enter *the with/against alternation, *the through/with alternation, *the conative alternation, the body-part possessor ascension alternation, *the causative alternation, the instrument subject alternation, and the Resultative phrase. Touch verbs are pure verbs of contact; they describe surface contact with no necessary implication that the contact came about through physical contact. This class of verbs show a more limited range of properties than the Verbs of Contact by Impact which only allow intentional action interpretations with body-part or reflexive object (Levin 1993:154-155).

2.2.3 Problems in Levin's Study

Levin (1993) does an extensive job in data collection and classifies verbs according to their syntactic behavior. Her job sets a good foundation for the studies of verb-variant relations, but there are still some problems in her research.

Firstly, some typical variants which make differences in the study of verb-variant relations are neglected by Levin. According to the data of this thesis, the variants expressing direction, location and possession change in forms of propositional phrases or ditransitive structures are characteristic of physical contact verbs, which Levin fails to distinguish, for example:

a. He knocked the man <u>to the ground</u>.

(http://www.femalefirst.co.uk/entertainment/Adrian+Pasdar-43012.html)

b. I hit the ball <u>into the net</u>.

(http://www.actionscript.org/forums/showthread.php3?t=79508)

c. I hit a ball <u>to him</u>.

(http://answers.yahoo.com/question/index?qid=20080302180556AAkI04e)

d. I hit <u>him a ball</u>.

(http://www.oprah.com/relationships/How-to-Get-Good-at-Love/5)

In example *a*, the propositional phrases *to the ground* expresses the direction change caused by the knock action; the propositional phrases *into the net* in example b expresses change in location; the propositional phrases *to him* in example c expresses the possession change; and the ditransitive structure *hit him a ball* express the possession change.

Besides, according the data of this thesis, two variants expressing change in property are distinguished, i.e., that in form of adjective phrase and that in form of propositional phrase, For example:

I always bumped the door <u>open.</u>

(http://fattygoesrunning.blogspot.com/2010/11/fatty-runs-to-gym.html)

I think I bumped him <u>to death</u>.

(http://www.textnovel.com/error.php)

Levin only distinguished the former variant.

Secondly, the definitions of some alternations are fussy. For example, the with alternation, against alternation, and the through alternation obviously have different structures, express different meanings, and emphasize different aspects, but Levin defined them as with/against alternation and through/with alternation. It is difficult for readers to understand.

Thirdly, there exists improperness in the division of subgroups. For example, in terms of lexical meaning, *punch* and *swat* in subclass 18.2 are obviously more close to the Hit verb than to the Swat verb; and *bite, claw, scratch, peck*, and *stab* have a close connection with the Poke verbs of class 19. These can be fairly justified by the corpus of this thesis and would be illustrated in chapter 3.

Fourthly, the meaning of physical contact verbs defined by Levin under Lexical semantics is coarse-grained with some of the semantic details of physical contact event being excluded by her definition. For instance, the meaning components of actor, instrument, object and the possible changes are not included in the definition.

Moreover, Levin does not pay attention to the minute differences in the meaning of variants caused by different participants. For example:

He hit the <u>stick</u> against the fence.

(http://www.wordwizard.com/phpbb3/viewtopic.php?f=16&t=22570&p=76204)

Jack hit the <u>ball</u> against the fence.

(http://www.jstor.org/stable/25001247)

The two sentences have the same syntactic structure but they emphasize different participants of the action. The former emphasizes the change in the instrument '*stick*', while the latter emphasizes the change in the object '*ball*'. Another set of examples are:

He hit the fence.

(http://www.naderlibrary.com/dick.preservmachine4.htm)

The stick hit the fence.

(http://www.reference-global.com/doi/abs/10.1515/ling.1990.28.6.1201)

Once the ball hit the fence, it became a bounding ball.

(http://books.google.com.hk/books?id=1ioDAAAAMBAJ&pg=PA73&lpg=PA73&dq=%22The+ba
ll+hit+the+fence%22&source=bl&ots=4OLFmJy6iT&sig=Z20ziE1LNNswS922YClJsVIQadY&hl=zh-
CN&ei=isS4TeO8MZGYvAOz3vGiAw&sa=X&oi=book_result&ct=result&resnum=8&ved=0CGoQ6A
EwBw#v=onepage&q=%22The%20ball%20hit%20the%20fence%22&f=false)

This set of sentences share the same syntactic structure, but they take actor, instrument, and object as topic respectively which are the emphasis of the sentences.

These problems reveal that the classification and analysis of verbs merely on the basis of syntactic behavior is coarse-grained and inexact. As a consequence, the introduction of approaches that can refine the classification and the semantic analysis of physical contact verbs is necessary.

2.3 Construction Grammar

2.3.1 Goldberg's Construction Grammar

A central thesis of Construction Grammar (Goldberg, 1995, 2010) is that basic sentences in English are instances of constructions---form-meaning correspondences that exist independent of particular verbs, that is, constructions themselves carry meaning, independent of the words (word meanings) of the sentence.

Construction Grammar (Goldberg, 1995, 2010) believes that subtle semantic and pragmatic factors are critical in understanding the constraints imposed on grammatical constructions. These ideas in many respects hearken back to Generative Semantics. Construction Grammar absorbs some ideas from Frame Semantics (Fillmore 1968, 1982, 1997) which is an approach to language based on human experiences (Lakoff, 1987, 2014) and an approach to semantics which recognizes the importance of speaker-centered "construal" of situations in the sense of Langacker (1987, 1990, 1991).

In Construction Grammar (Goldberg, 1995, 2010), no strict division is set up between lexicon and syntax. Both are considered as the declaratively represented data structure. Another notion rejected here is that of a strict division between semantics and pragmatics. Information about focused constitutes, topicality, and register is represented in constructions alongside semantic information.

In her monograph *Constructions: A Construction Grammar Approach to Argument Structure* (Goldberg, 1995, 2010), Goldberg explores the idea that argument structure constructions are a special subclass of constructions that provides the basic means of clausal expression in a language.

On a constructional approach to argument structure, syntactic differences in meaning between the same verbs in different constructions are attributed directly to the particular constructions. We will see that if we consider various constructions on their own terms, interesting generations and subtle semantic constrains emerge.

According to Construction Grammar, a distinct construction is defined to exist if one or more of its properties are not strictly predictable from knowledge of other constructions existing in the grammar:

C is a COSTRUCTION if C is a form-meaning pair <Fi,Si> such that some aspect of Fi or some aspect of Si is not strictly predictable from C's component parts or from other previously established constructions.

Constructions are taken to be the basic units of language. Phrasal patterns and morphemes are all considered constructions only if they fit the above criteria of construction. The collection of constructions is taken to constitute a highly structured lattice of interrelated information. Linguistic constructions display prototype structure and form networks of associations.

It is hypothesized that:

Simple clause constructions are associated directly with semantic structures which reflect scenes basic to human experience.

In particular, constructions involving basic argument structure are shown to be associated with dynamic scenes: experientially grounded gestalts. It is proposed that the basic clause types of a language form an interrelated network, with semantic structures paired with particular forms as general a way as possible (Goldberg 1995:1-7).

The argument structure constructions discussed by Goldberg include:

Ditransitive	X CAUSES Y TO RECEIVE Z	Subj V Obj Obj2 Pat faxed Bill the letter.
Caused Motion	X CAUSES Y TO MOVE Z	Subj V Obj Obl Pat sneezed the napkin off the table.
Resultative	X CAUSES Y TO BECOME Z	Subj V Obj Xcomp She kissed him unconscious.

Intrans. Motion	X MOVES Y	Subj V Obl The fly buzzed into the room.
Conative	X DIRECTS ACTION AT Y	Subj V Obl_at Sam kicked at Bill.

2.3.2 The Interaction between Verbs and Constructions

According to Goldberg (1995, 2010)'s viewpoint, if basic sentence types are viewed as argument structure constructions and the same verb is involved in more than one construction, the following questions need to be dealt with: 1) What is the nature of verb meaning? 2) What is the nature of construction meaning? 3) When can a given verb occur in a given construction?

In Goldberg (1995, 2010)'s theory, verbs, as well as nouns, involve frame semantic meanings; that is, their designation must include the reference to a background frame rich with world and cultural knowledge. Verbs lexically determine which aspects of their frame semantic knowledge are profiled and the differences in the expressions of their arguments can be accounted for by a semantic difference in profiling. Constructions are typically associated with a family of closely related senses rather than a single, fixed abstract sense. A construction has a fairly specific central sense and postulating separate related senses which make reference to specific verb classes.

Constructions must specify in which ways verbs will combine with them; they need to be able to constrain the class of verbs that can be integrated with them in various ways and must specify the way in which the event type designated by the verb is integrated into the event type designated by the construction. If a verb is a member of a verb class that is conventionally associated with a construction, then the participant roles of the verb may be semantically fused with argument roles of the argument structure construction. "Fusion" is meant here to capture the simultaneous semantic constrains on the participant roles associated with the verb and the argument roles of the construction. The result of integrating the verb with the construction must be an event type (E) that is itself construable as a single event. (Goldberg 1995:24-65).

2.3.3 Goldberg's Study of Verbs

The present book would take the physical contact verbs as examples to test the effectiveness of Construction Gramma (Goldberg, 1995, 2010) in classifying English verbs and in analyzing the relation between verbs and their constructions.

Based on Construction Grammar, basic sentences in English are instances of constructions---form-meaning correspondences that exist independently of particular verbs (Goldberg 1995:1). Syntactic differences in meaning between the same verbs in different constructions are attributed directly to the particular constructions (Goldberg 1995:4). Verbs, as well as nouns, involve frame semantic meanings, that is, their designation must make reference to a background frame which includes world and cultural knowledge. Constructions must specify in which way verbs will combine with them; they need to be able to constrain the classes of verbs that can be integrated with them in various ways and must specify the way in which the event type designated by the verb is integrated into the event type designated by the construction (Goldberg 1995:27)

Five argument structure constructions are discussed by Goldberg. An analysis of physical contact verbs under Construction Grammar is done by the writer (see Appendix3: Distribution of Physical Contact Verbs in Constructions).

(1) **Ditransitive Construction** (Subj+ V+ Obj+ Obj2): its central sense involves successful transfer between a volitional agent and a willing recipient (X causes Y to receive Z), for example, *Sally baked her sister a cake*. The meaning of 'intended transition' is characteristic of this construction and one must consider the verb *bake* as including the meaning of 'X causes Y to receive Z through the intended action of bake'. And through the metaphorical mechanism of the system, the central meaning can be expended, for example: *She told Joe a tale. / She blew him a kiss.* The constraints set by the construction for the entry of verbs are: the independent choice of a voluntary subject argument by the verb and the animations of the first object (Goldberg 1995:141-151).

The verbs *hit, knock, kick, tap* and *slam* from the Verbs of Contact by Physical contact in Levin's classification can enter this construction; most Poke verbs and Touch verbs (except *pinch* and *tickle*) can not enter this construction.

(2) **Caused Motion Construction** (Subj V Obj Obl): its basic meaning is that the causer argument directly causes the theme argument to move along a path designated by the directional phrase (X causes Y to move Z). This basic meaning is extended in various ways, allowing the construction to appear with a variety of systematically related interpretations, for example: *You bump the ball to your teammates.* The evidence for its existence as a construction is that several aspects of the meaning of caused motion expressions (causation, motion) and of their form (e.g., the direct object complement) are not generally predictable from lexical requirements or from other constructions. The semantic constraints from this construction can be interpreted as beginning to provide necessary conditions on the notion of 'direct

18

causation' (Goldberg 1995:152-179).

The physical contact verbs that have an entry to this construction are: Hit verbs of 18.1 (except *drum* and *rap)*, Non-Agentive verbs of 18.4, Poke verbs, and Touch verbs; Swat verbs of 18.2 (except *hammer* and *stab*) and Spank verbs of 18.3 can not enter this construction.

(3) **Resultative Construction** (Subj V Obj Xcomp): this construction, with the central meaning of 'X causes Y to become Z', is considered as a metaphorical extension of the Caused-motion construction. The necessary constraint on the appearance of resultatives can be predicted in semantic terms: the resultative can only apply to patient arguments that potentially undergo a change of state as a result of the action denoted by the verb (Goldberg 1995:180). The semantic constrains were proposed in order to restrict the applicability of the lexical rule: the existence of an instigator argument; the causation involved must be direct; the resultative adjective must have a clearly delimited lower bound and must be considered a type of path phrase, which accounts for several co-occurrence restrictions (Goldberg 1995:198).

Among the Spank verbs of 18.3, only *cane, knife* and *whip* enter this construction. Among the other subclasses, most of the physical contact verbs (except *bump, kick, rap, brush, touch, kiss, pinch* and *tickle*) can not enter this construction.

(4) **Intrans. Motion Construction** (Subj V Obl): its central meaning is X moves Y. Almost all the physical contact verbs studied in this thesis (except *strap, cane, brain,* and *conk*) can enter this construction.

(5) **Conative Construction** (Subj V Obl$_{at}$): its central meaning is X directs action at Y. All the physical contact verbs studied in this thesis can enter this construction.

The five argument constructions discussed in Construction Grammar can cover the constructions physical contact verbs have access to enter. Through the analysis of the distribution of physical contact verbs in constructions, we can get a brief picture of the constraints imposed by constructions to physical contact verbs in their integration with the constructions. The constructions discussed in this approach and the idea of extending the meaning of basic constructions do enlighten other studies in form-meaning relations, including Cognitive-Functional Approach.

But there are problems in the study of physical contact verbs under Construction Grammar which indicate that it's not an efficient approach in such application.

2.3.4 Problems Goldberg's Study

Firstly, the classification of physical contact verbs according to their distributions in constructions is inefficient. The major differences in the distributions of physical contact verbs are: only a small part of

Hit verbs (*hit, knock, kick, tap* and *smack*) can enter Ditransitive construction, and Poke verbs, Touch verbs, Swat verbs, Spank verbs and Non-Agentive verbs do not have access to enter this construction; most of the Swat verbs and Spank verbs (except *conk, hammer* and *stab*) can't enter Caused Motion construction. Merely through such differentiations, the classification of physical contact verbs is an impossible work.

Secondly, the descriptions of the meaning of certain constructions are improper. For example, the central meaning of Caused Motion construction is "X causes Y to Move Z", but according to the structure of "Subj V Obj Obl (*Pat sneezed the napkin off the table*)" it is more proper to define the meaning as "X causes Y to Move to Z"; Also, according to the structure of Intrans. Motion construction: "Subj V Obl (*The fly buzzed into the room*)", the central meaning of this construction "X moves Y" should be redefined as 'X Moves to Z".

Thirdly, the definition of the meaning of Caused Motion construction does not include all the meanings this construction expresses. This construction is defined as "X causes Y to Move Z" (according to writer's view, it should be modified as "X causes Y to Move to Z"), but the following sentences are all belong to this construction, with each having a different meaning.

a. Some players use their heads to try to hit the ball <u>into</u> the net.

(http://www.ryedu.net/syy/seyy/200807/8264_2.html)

b. He hit his forehead <u>against</u> the kerb when he fell (Zhang, 2003).

c. He hit the ball <u>off</u> the table.

(http://www.mtv.com/news/articles/1530131/rockstar-games-hosts-table-tennis-battles.jhtml)

The Obl component in the construction can be expressed by *into, against, off,* and other propositional phrases. But each of them has a subtle different meaning. For instance, *into* expresses "X causes Y to move into Z"; *against* expresses "X causes Y to move to Z, and Z gives Y certain counterforce"; *off* expresses 'X causes Y to move out of Z'. As a consequence, the central meaning of the Caused Motion construction should be "X causes Y to move to\into\out of Z (with Z gives Y certain counterforce in some conditions)".

Fourthly, there are sentence structures belonging to one construction bear the meaning feature of another construction, for example:

a. Some players use their heads to try to hit the ball <u>into</u> the net.

b. You should hit the ball <u>at</u> the wall.

(http://www.sportscomet.com/Volleyball/227806.htm)

These two sentences both belong to Caused Motion construction and the "caused motion" are represented by *into* and *at* propositional phrase respectively. *Into* phrase does express "caused motion", while *at* phrase obviously bears the meaning of "conative" which is one of the characteristics of Conative construction.

Another instance is:

a. Some players use their heads to try to hit the ball <u>into</u> the net.

b. Taro hit the glass <u>into</u> three pieces.

(http:// books.google.com.hk/books?isbn=1405114851...)

These two sentences both belong Caused Motion construction, but the sentence a bears the meaning of 'caused motion' and sentence b bears the meaning of 'resultative' which is characteristic of the Resultative construction.

Fifthly, the sentence components in the same position of the construction may bear different emphases, which can not be distinguished merely through the analysis of construction meaning. For example:

a. He hit the <u>stick</u> to the ground.

(http://watervole.livejournal.com/444689.html)

b. When you hit the <u>ball</u> to the ground, the ball bounces in an unpredictable way.

(http://www.nextag.com/tennis-hit-a-way/stores-html)

Stick and *ball* are both in the object position of the construction, but the use of *stick* in the construction emphasizes the change in location of the instrument while the use of *ball* emphasizes the change in location of the patient.

In conclusion, the problems arise in the study of physical contact verbs under the Construction Grammar (1995, 2010) indicate that it is inefficient in such application and more precise and effective approaches are called for.

2.4 Cognitive-Functional Approach

Cheng (2002, 2005, 2006, 2019, 2020) constructed the "Conceptual Frame", later developed into the "Cognitive Event Frame" to theoretically formulate the conceptual content of clause/events, which is considered to be the connection part between the sensory-motor system and the linguistic expression system. This approach emphasizes the experiential knowledge stored in the brain and the inseparability of the encyclopedia knowledge with the lexical meaning of verbs (Cheng 2006:48). Under this approach, conceptual meaning (in the brain) forms with grammatical structure embodiment relation through grammatical meaning, and grammatical meaning becomes the transition between such embodiment relation (Cheng 2006: 71); in this way, the form-meaning relation is turned into the relation between form (grammatical structure) and brain (conceptual meaning).

2.4.1 The Cognitive-Functional Approach

Following Neurocognitive Linguistics (Lamb, 1966, 1999) and making references to other linguistic approaches, such as the Cognitive Semantics (Talmy, 1991, 2000a, 2000b), the Cognitive Grammar (Langacker, 1987, 1990, 1991) and the Systematic Functional Grammar (Halliday, 1994), Cheng (2002, 2005, 2006) proposed the Cognitive-Functional Approach of linguistic study. This approach focuses mainly on the relationship between conceptual meaning and syntactic expression as well as the mental operation of linguistic system. It aims at describing and interpreting the semiotic embodiment relation between meaning and expression.

The main characteristics of Cognitive-Functional Approach are (Cheng, 2006: 48-49): Cognitive-Functional Approach is a model of semiotic relational system which includes the conceptual semantic system and the lexical grammatical system; 2) The conceptual content in the semiotic relationship should be encyclopedic; 3) This approach holds that the physical container of such system is the neurophysiological system in the brain, and the mental representation should not go against the neurophysiological reality; 4) The Cognitive-Functional Approach addresses both the relation of connectedness and the process of activating; 5) The research scope of this model is the entire linguistic system and its operation, rather than the restricted "innate" Universal Grammar; 6) This approach takes the relational notation set by Lamb (1966, 1999) as the basic type of linking relationship and attempts to maintain the operational feasibility and neurophysiological feasibility.

The main objective of the Cognitive-Functional Approach is to formulate and explain language system residing in the human brain. Lamb (1966, 1999) reveals that language is physiologically based on the neural network in the brain. Linguistic system is not in itself a symbol system at all, but a network of relationship. Neurocognitive Linguistics believes that building models is one of our automatic mental activities. Based on the viewpoint that "we have to adopt an indirect approach, called modeling", the Cognitive-Functional Approach attempts to set up a model which can formulate and interpret the relationship between expression and meaning.

Cognitive-Functional Approach emphasizes the encyclopedia knowledge stored in human brain and the inseparability of such encyclopedia knowledge with lexical meaning of verbs. According to Cheng's viewpoint, the use and understanding of verbs would arouse schematic effect, that is, the mental processing of the meaning of verbs would activate the relevant schemata in the brain, which are composed of encyclopedia knowledge. And there exist a connection between the perceptual-locomotor system and the linguistic expression system, and the joint between them is the conceptual meaning system, which is a kind of schema. (Cheng, 2002, 2005, 2006)

In various approaches, the research of meaning is concerned with two parts: the conceptual meaning and the grammatical meaning (including the syntactic meaning). In the Cognitive-Functional Approach, the conceptual meaning system is a cognitive, social, and encyclopedic meaning system which takes neural network as its physiological container. The Conceptual meaning forms with the grammatical structure representational relation through grammatical meaning, and the grammatical meaning becomes the transition between such representational relation (Cheng 2006: 71). As a consequence, under this approach, the research of the semantic correspondence between verbs and their constructions (grammatical structures) would be illustrated through the exploration of the representational relation between the conceptual meanings and the linguistic expressions.

2.4.2 The Conceptual Frame

In the Cognitive-Functional Approach, the mechanism of Conceptual Frame is used to "formally represent the conceptual content (conceptual meaning) of clauses", which forms with the linguistic expression embodiment relation (Cheng 2006:1). In Cognitive-Functional Approach, the notion of Conceptual Frame is defined as the "formal representation of the conceptual content of clauses" and it connects with the linguistic expression to form semiotic relationship. The cognitive significances of the conceptual frame are: its semiotic relationship, i.e., its embodiment relation with grammatical structure, and its operational feasibility. It does not go against the physiological feasibility (Cheng 2006: 1).

The encyclopedic feature of conceptual meaning can deduce its diversity which is indispensable in understanding clauses (Goldberg, 1995, 2010). For example:

Avoid touching the crack by skipping over it.

?? Avoid touching the crack by crawling over it

To explain the differences between these two sentences the lexicon meaning is powerless since their conceptual meanings are different: the action concerned with *skip* is not in touch with the object while that concerned with *crawl* would inevitably touch the object. To explain the distribution of verbs in sentence structures in terms of conceptual meaning is more precise. (Cheng 2006: 72-74).

Based on the relation between an object and an object being referred to, the conceptual semantic domains (Conceptual Domains in short) are defined which are parts of conceptual meaning system. The physical and mental domains are distinguished, each of which is divided into location, possession and property domain respectively. There is cross-domain semiotic similarity between physical and mental domain because location, possession and property in these two domains have similarities in grammatical structures (Cheng 2006: 80-82).

Conceptual frame is composed of conceptual meaning structures (Conceptual Structures in short), which are the structures to express conceptual meanings. Different combinations of these conceptual structures form different conceptual frames. The substances in the world form three kinds of relations: spatio-temperal existential relation, action relation and causative relation, and they are expressed by three kinds of conceptual structures: the spatio-temperal structure which represents the state of existence of the object; the action structure which represents the action event; and the causation structure which represents the causative relation. Every conceptual domain includes these three kinds of conceptual structures (Cheng 2006: 94-97).

According to the Cognitive-Functional Approach, the essence of conceptual frame is a local relational network with certain motivating and linking value. The reason why the conceptual meaning of a clause is represented as the conceptual frame is that one clause may be composed of several conceptual structures, that is, one clause can motivate several conceptual structures. Conceptual frame is composed of three parts: the condition is an assumption of the state whose truth is taken for granted in discourse; the post-condition is the linguistic implication; the conceptual process is the core of the frame and represents the events and the states of the conceptual content in the course of time. The conceptual process begins with the end of the condition and stops at the beginning of the post-condition. It represents the main conceptual content, and condition and post-conditon is the extension of the activation of conceptual process (Cheng 2006:97-99). For example, the conceptual frame of the clause *They hit the bottle broken* is:

Condition	[Object bottle +State broken] + Negative
Process	Causer they +Cause +Object bottle +trend[Object bottle +Final State broken]
	Actor they + Act hit +Object bottle
Post-condition	Object bottle +State broken

A conceptual frame typically consists of a network of mutually activated clauses, each of which activates different aspects of the frame and thus is realized by distinct grammatical structures. Partial activation of a conceptual frame will leave the whole frame semi-activated.

2.4.3 The Cognitive Event Frame

The conceptual frame is designed as the "formal representation of the conceptual content/meaning of clauses", which forms with the linguistic expression embodiment relation (Cheng, 2002, 2005, 2006); and the conceptual content/meaning bears an encyclopedic feature (Goldberg, 1995, 2010). In essence, the conceptual frame of one type of event formulates the experiences related with that type of event, which are stored in the brain as the conceptual content/meaning. Cheng (2019, 2020) further developed this formulation system from conceptual frame into Cognitive Event Frame, not only by changing the title, but also by elaborating the system.

Under the Cognitive Event Frame approach, the brain-stored experiential knowledge network concerned with one type of event is called the conceptual content of that type of event. The conceptual content of one type of event could be classified as the "elaborated conceptual content" and the "core conceptual content", with the former including the latter. The Core Conceptual Content describes the part of the experiential knowledge network that all the sensory-motor practices belonging to one type of event would involve and the processing of any construction of this type of event would activate; it can be formulated by the "Core Cognitive Event Frame". The Elaborated Conceptual Content should be able to conclude all the elements and the complete processes of different sensory-motor practices belonging to one type of event and can completely describe the whole experiential knowledge network of this type of event; it can be formulated as the "Elaborated Cognitive Event Frame".

According to the Cognitive Event Frame approach, the experiences gained from different sensory-motor practices form different paths of the experiential knowledge network of one type of event in the brain, and these experiences would be construed as different verbs and constructions in language usage; the processing of different language information (structure) would also activate different paths of the experiential knowledge network of this type of event, which in turn activate related sensory-motor experiences. Different constructions of one type of event express specific conceptual meaning, but share the core conceptual content of this type of event (Cheng & Zhang, 2012).

2.4.4 Advantages and Disadvantages of the Cognitive Event Frame Approach

In this approach, conceptual meaning (in the brain) forms with grammatical structure representational relation through grammatical meaning, and grammatical meaning becomes the transition between such representative relation (Cheng 2006: 71), consequently, the form-meaning relation is turned into the relation between form (grammatical structure) and brain (conceptual meaning). Although the Cognitive Event Frame approach did not include the level of body (the sensory-motor system) in its form (grammatical structure) — brain (conceptual meaning) representative system, this approach has paid attention to the connection between the sensory-motor system and the language expression system revolving around the brain network of experiential knowledge, which is in line with the viewpoint of the Embodied Language of Cognition (Glenberg, 1997; Barsalou, 1999; Anderson, 2003). Besides, the Cognitive Event Frame approach could formulize the content of the experiential knowledge stored in the brain, which is economical in description; and its explanation of the construction-construal mechanism does not violate the feasibility of the neural operation of the language system (Cheng, 2019, 2020).

2.5 Summary

Many theories of Cognitive Linguistics, such as Semantic Structure (Jackendoff, 1990, 2002, 2007), Cognitive Semantics (Talmy, 1991; 2000a; 2000b), Construction Grammar (Goldberg, 1995, 2010), Cognitive Grammar (Langacker, 1987, 1990, 1991), and Metaphor Theory (Lakoff, 1987, 2014), have had the idea of analyzing language by connecting to the functions of brain cognition. These theories concerned about the conceptual meaning in the brain that based on human experiences, however, none of them pay attention to the sensory-motor system, which is the basis of human experiences.

Levin (1993) does an extensive job in data collection and made classification of verbs according to their syntactic behavior. Her research provides a good foundation for the studies of verb-construction relations, but there are problems in her study. Firstly, some typical variants which make differences in the study of verb-variant relations are neglected. Secondly, the definitions of certain variants are fussy. Thirdly, certain improperness exists in the division of subgroups. Fourthly, the meaning of physical contact verbs defined by Levin under Lexical semantics is coarse-grained with some of the semantic details of physical contact event being excluded by her definition. Fifthly, Levin does not pay attention to the minute differences in the meaning of variants caused by different participants.

The constructions discussed in Construction Grammar (Goldberg, 1995, 2010) and the idea of extending the meaning of basic constructions do enlighten other studies in form-meaning relations, but this approach has certain problems in the study of verb-construction relations. Firstly, the classification of physical contact verbs according to their distributions in constructions is ineffective. Secondly, the descriptions of the meaning of certain constructions are improper. Thirdly, the definition of the meaning of Caused Motion construction does not include all the meanings this construction expresses. Fourthly, there are sentence structures belonging to one construction bear the meaning feature of another construction. Fifthly, the sentence components in the same position of the construction may bear different emphases, which can not be distinguished merely through the analysis of construction meaning.

Under the Cognitive Event Frame approach, conceptual meaning (in the brain) forms with grammatical structure representational relation through grammatical meaning, and grammatical meaning becomes the transition between such representative relation (Cheng 2006: 71), consequently, the form-meaning relation is turned into the relation between form (grammatical structure) and brain (conceptual meaning). Although the Cognitive Event Frame approach did not include the level of body (the sensory-motor system) in its form (grammatical structure) — brain (conceptual meaning) representative system, this approach has paid attention to the connection between the sensory-motor system and the language expression system, jointing by the brain network of experiential knowledge.

Chapter Three Theoretical Hypothesis: The "Body—Brain—Form" Three-dimensional Approach

The perspective of the Embodied Cognition, which is a new research approach of cognitive science proposed on the bases of abundant neuro-cognitive evidence, suggests that "cognition is a kind of highly embodied, scenario-based activities; it is also a kind of experiences depending on certain prototypes and generated from the interaction between one's body and its environment" (Anderson, 2003). The perspective of the Embodied Language of Cognition suggests that language roots in the human sensory-motor system, emphasizing the function of experiences (Glenberg, 1997; Barsalou, 1999); it is further proposed that language processing are the mental simulation processes of the operation of the sensory-motor system and related experiences (Guan, 2007).

A lot of Neurolinguistic studies (Martin et al., 1996; Tettamanti et al, 2005; Zwaan, 2006; Whiteny, 2009) found that in different levels of language processing, i.e., no matter in word, sentence, or in discourse processing, the related perceptual, (muscular) movement, and other experiential traces would all be activated, supporting the viewpoints of the Embodied Language of Cognition (Glenberg, 1997; Barsalou, 1999). For example, to process the sentence "*Take the ice-cream from the refrigerator*", the processor need to activate the knowledge of related movement experience (i.e., to take the ice-cream and to feel its quality) and that of related perceptual experience (i.e., to see the ice-cream, to smell it, and to feel its coldness), that is, to process the sentence, the processor need to extract related experiential memory, and the extraction of the memory would activate the sensory-motor system related with real taking, seeing, smelling, and feeling practices.

Under the perspective of the Embodied Language of Cognition (Glenberg, 1997; Barsalou, 1999; Anderson, 2003), this book proposes a theoretical hypothesis: the form-meaning relation in language shall be a three-dimensional interactive relation between body (the sensory-motor system) — brain (the mental network of the experiential knowledge) — form (the language expression system), rather than be a two dimensional relation between meaning and form. The language users get experiences about the world through sensory-motor practices of the bodies; these experiential memories are processed, integrated, and stored in the brain, which form the brain network system of experiential knowledge; the experiential knowledge in the brain functions in language usage and interrelates with lexical-syntactical structures to turn into specific language expressions. At the same time, the processing of specific language information and structures need to extract the part of the brain experiential knowledge related with the language content (meaning), and the extraction of this part of the experiential knowledge would activate the part of the sensory-motor system related with this part of experiences.

Under the "Body—Brain—Form" three-dimensional approach, the specific "meaning" comes from the body (the sensory-motor practices), (which become a part of the experiential knowledge) stored in the brain, and embodied as certain language form (expression); at the same time, the processing of certain language expression needs to extract the "meaning" (related experiential knowledge) from the brain, which in turn actives the "meaning" (related sensory-motor experiences) from the body. The brain is the core of the three-dimensional interactive relation, which joints the body and the language expression.

The theoretical hypothesis of the "body—brain—form" three-dimensional relation has not been systematically studied and tested. Cognitive linguistics focuses on language usage (Lamb, 1966, 1999). Since the core of the "body—brain—form" three-dimensional relation is the brain, to test the feasibility of this approach, we shall consider whether it can theoretically describe the conceptual content/meaning in the brain, i.e., the mental network of the experiential knowledge, and whether it can effectively explain the cognitive operation as well as the usage-distribution of the language system.

As a consequence, the main objective of the present book is to test the feasibility of the "body—brain—form" theoretical framework (hypothesis), i.e., to test whether it can effectively explain the cognitive operation and the usage-distribution of the language system. To address this issue, this book takes certain daily event, i.e., the obtaining event, as an example to explain the interaction between its sensory-motor practices, its brain experiential knowledge network, and the construal of its (English) constructions. Beside, this book would adopt the "Cognitive Event Frame" (Cheng, 2019, 2020) to formulate the brain experiential knowledge network (the conceptual content) of the obtaining event, which is an effective and economical tool in formulating conceptual contents. Moreover, this book would build corpuses of different types of obtaining verbs and constructions, and use quantitative analysis to test the effectiveness and accuracy of the "body—brain—form" approach in explaining the neural operation and the usage-distribution of the language system.

Besides the main objective, this book also reports several data analysis cases under the framework of the "Conceptual Frame" approach (Cheng, 2002, 2005, 2006) to further verify the effectiveness of this approach in formulating conceptual contents, including the analysis on the physical contact event and its (English) constructions and the comparative analysis on the throwing event and its Chinese and English constructions and that on the delivery event and its Chinese and English constructions.

Chapter Four The "Body—Brain—Form" Approach to Obtaining Event and Its Expressions

There are some events, such as the obtaining event, the delivery event, the throwing event, the communication event, and the physical contact event, that are parts of human daily activities. Different actions/practices belonging to one type of event would be processed, integrated, and stored in the brain to form the experiential knowledge network of this type of event and be construed as different verbs and constructions of this type of event in language usage. These events and their language expressions (i.e., verbs and constructions) are typical materials to test the neural feasibility and descriptive effectiveness of linguistic theories. As a consequence, the main objective of the present book is to test the feasibility of the "body—brain—form" theoretical framework (hypothesis), i.e., to test whether it can effectively explain the cognitive operation and the usage-distribution of the language system. To address this issue, this book takes certain daily event, i.e., the obtaining event, as an example to explain the interaction between its sensory-motor practices, its brain experiential knowledge network, and the construal of its (English) constructions. Beside, this book would adopt the "Cognitive Event Frame" (Cheng, 2019, 2020) to formulate the brain experiential knowledge network (the conceptual content) of the obtaining event, which is an effective and economical tool in formulating conceptual contents. Moreover, this book would build corpuses of different types of obtaining verbs and constructions, and use quantitative analysis to test the effectiveness and accuracy of the "body—brain—form" approach in explaining the neural operation and the usage-distribution of the language system.

4.1 The Corpus of Obtaining Verbs and Constructions

Levin (1993) made a classification of different categories of English verbs from a lexical-semantic perspective. This section chooses the 13.5 (Verbs of Obtaining) category and the 13.6 (Verbs of Exchange) category of verbs from Levin (1993), altogether 58 verbs, as the Obtaining Verbs studied in this book.

The corpus of Obtaining Verbs and Constructions is built according to the 5 steps reported in section 1.3 (Methodology of The Research). Altogether, the corpus collected 58 obtaining verbs and 336 obtaining constructions. Based on the specific conceptual meaning each construction bear, the obtaining constructions are classified into 18 categories (see 4.1.2 for detailed analysis). This section number and name these constructions, and do quantitative statistics to them (see Table 1 Statistic of obtaining constructions).

Table 1 Statistic of obtaining constructions

Subject	No.	Title	Example of the Construction	Frequency	Proportion(%)
Obtainer	1-1	Transitive Con.	They booked *a bedroom* there.	52	15.48
	1-2	Aim Con.	Our school chartered three buses *for the trip.*	42	12.50
	1-3	Price Con.	We bought it *with/for very little money.*	14	4.17
	1-4	Instrument Con.	He catch the ball *with both hands.*	16	4.76
	1-5	Approach Con.	Carmen booked a hotel *by/via email.*	30	8.93
	1-6	Location Con.	Carmen bought a dress *at/in Bloomingdale's.*	29	8.63
	1-7	Field Con.	Paul Getty acquired a fortune *in the oil business.*	12	3.57
	1-8-1	Exchange 1	*John and James* exchanged hats.	3	0.89
	1-8-2	Exchange 2	Mary exchanged seats *with Anne.*	5	1.49
	2-1	Original Owner	Carmen bought a dress *from Diana.*	23	6.85
	2-2	Original Location	The contractor earn fees *from the U.K.*	20	5.95
	2-3	Final Property	We chose Mr.Dick *as our leader.*	8	2.38
	3-1-1	Made Obtain 1	Carmen bought a dress *for Mary.*	36	10.71
	3-1-2	Made Obtain 2	Carmen bought *Mary a dress.*	29	8.63
Obtained-Object	4-1	(Obj) Transitive	*Honest politicians* cannot be bought.	5	1.49
	4-2	(Obj) Aim	The Hall was booked *for the meeting.*	3	0.89
	4-3	(Obj) Approach	Language can be acquired *by using it.*	1	0.30
	4-4	(Obj) Location	The cat was caught *in the trap.*	3	0.89
	4-5	(Obj) Original Owner	Leather is obtained *from animals.*	1	0.30
	4-6	(Obj) Original Location	The idea is stolen *from the United States.*	4	1.19
			Total	**336**	**100**

Note: Subject marks the subject/theme of the constructions; No. marks the number of different types of constructions; Title marks the title of different types of construction; For specific titles, Con. represent "construction", with the titles longer than two words Con. being omitted. Frequency marks the frequency of occurrence of a type of construction in all the 336 obtaining constructions; Proportion marks the proportion of a type of construction in all the obtaining constructions.

4.2 Obtaining Event and Its Cognitive Event Frames

4.2.1 The Core Conceptual Content and The Core Cognitive Event Frame of Obtaining Event

In the *Oxford Advanced Learner's English-Chinese Dictionary* (the 7th edition, 2009), the definition of "obtain" is "to get something, especially by making an effort". This definition omitted the subject and the object of the sentence, but still described the core conceptual content of the obtaining event: the actor (i.e., the obtainer) obtains or gets something (i.e., the obtained object) (from other people, i.e., the original owner of the obtained object). This is the part of the experiential knowledge network related with all the obtaining practices and the processing of any obtaining construction would activate.

From the sensory-motor aspect, the obtaining event includes at least two participants, i.e., the obtainer and the obtained object; and in language, these two participants shall be construed as the necessary elements of most of the obtaining constructions. The quantitative analysis of the data reveals that 94.94% (319/336) of the obtaining constructions contain these two elements; only 5.06% (17/336) of the obtaining constructions just include the obtained object, omitting the obtainer (in order to highlight the obtained object or because of the lacking of the obtainer). Besides, the obtaining event implies another participant, i.e., the original owner of the obtained object (original owner for short). Since the obtaining event emphasizes "obtaining" and weakens "giving", in the construal of the constructions the original owner is not a necessary element. According to the data quantitative analysis, only 14.29% (48/336) of the obtaining constructions include the element of original owner. Please compare the following two sentences:

She Obtainer had found a situation Obtained Object. (Transitive Construction)

Carmen Obtainer bought a dress Obtained Object from Diana Original Owner. (Original Owner Construction)

The core conceptual content of the obtaining event inevitably contains the concept of an obtaining action, that is, the action done by the obtainer, which might cause the transfer of the possession from the original owner to the obtainer. The implied concept of "change of possession" may not be overtly expressed in the construal of obtaining constructions. Besides, since the final owner of the obtained object coincides with the obtainer and is overtly expressed as the subject/theme of the obtaining construction, the concept of the possession-transfer from the original owner could be specifically construed as the "Original Owner Construction" in language usage, expressed by the propositional phrase *from...*; but the concept of the possession-transfer to the obtainer or the result of the transfer is not overtly expressed generally, that is, the obtaining event does not have a typical "Final Possession/ Location Construction". (see Figure 1 Core obtaining cognitive event frame)

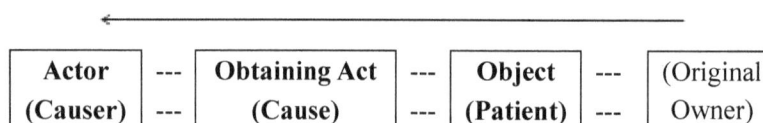

| Actor (Causer) | --- --- | Obtaining Act (Cause) | --- --- | Object (Patient) | --- --- | (Original Owner) |

Fig. 1 Core obtaining cognitive event frame

The Core Conceptual Content of the obtaining event could be formulated as the "Core Obtaining Cognitive Event Frame" (see Figure 1). The dotted lines in the frame represent the connection between the participants of the event; the arrow represents the transferring direction of the possession; the bold fonts and the non-bold ones represent the necessary and unnecessary activated elements, respectively; the brackets represent unnecessary overt expression of the element in construction construal. In the frame, the actor (obtainer) coincides with the causer of object change and the object of the action (the obtained object) coincides with the changed object (i.e., the patient of the action).

4.2.2 The Elaborated Conceptual Content and The Elaborated Cognitive Event Frame of Obtaining Event

The elaborated conceptual content of the obtaining event should be able to conclude all the elements and the complete processes of different sensory-motor practices of obtaining and can completely describe the whole experiential knowledge network of the obtaining event. Combining specific sensory-motor practices of obtaining actions, the elaborated conceptual content of the obtaining event can be conclude as: for some purposes, the actor (i.e., the obtainer) obtains or gets something (i.e., the obtained object) from other people or location (i.e., the original owner or location of the obtained object), by certain approach, using certain instrument (one's body or outer instrument), or paying certain price; this would cause the change of the possession of the obtained object and may cause the change of location or property of the object; sometimes, the obtaining purpose may be realized by exchange". The elaborated conceptual content of the obtaining event could be formulated as the "Elaborated Cognitive Event Frame" (see figure 2). The dotted lines in the frame represent the connection between the participants of the event; the arrow represents the transferring direction of the possession; the round brackets and square brackets represent unnecessary overt expression of the elements in construction construal, the slashes represent optional relations.

The elaborated conceptual event frame of the obtaining event contains the content expressed by the core conceptual event frame. Different sensory-motor practices of obtaining are formulated as different elements in the elaborated conceptual event frame and are construed as different obtaining verbs and constructions. The Processing of different obtaining constructions would activate different paths of the obtaining knowledge network in the brain, which were formulated as different elements of the elaborated conceptual event frame, and in turn activate specific obtaining sensory-motor experiences.

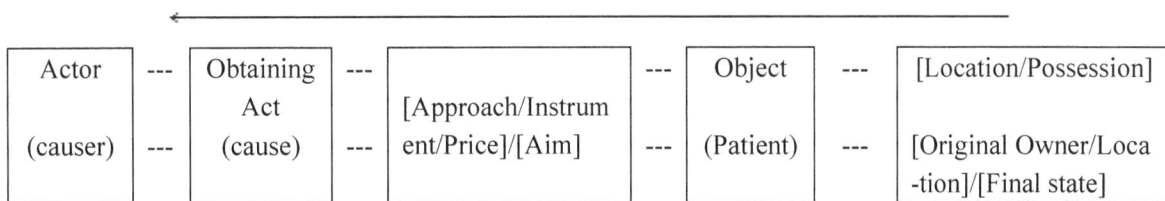

Actor	---	Obtaining Act	---		---	Object	---	[Location/Possession]
(causer)	---	(cause)	---	[Approach/Instrument/Price]/[Aim]	---	(Patient)	---	[Original Owner/Loca-tion]/[Final state]

Fig. 2 Elaborated obtaining cognitive event frame

The core conceptual event frame and the elaborated conceptual event frame of the obtaining event both composed of two levels of conceptual structures, i.e., the action conceptual structure (the upper level) and the causing to change conceptual structure (the lower level), representing the concept of the obtaining actions and the concept of the changes done to the object, respectively. According to the level of conceptual structures different obtaining sensory-motor practices correspond to, obtaining experiences are construed as two main categories of constructions: the transitive category and the change of object category.

(1) The transitive category of obtaining constructions

This category of constructions just emphasize the concept of "the obtaining actions having certain effect to the object of the action", and weakened the concept of the change of the object; the action conceptual structure in the cognitive event frame is activated and the causing to change conceptual structure is not activated. The transitive obtaining constructions could be classified into 8 types (see construction 1-1 to 1-8-2 in Table 1). In the "Transitive Construction", just the actor and the object of the obtaining action are activated. In the "Aim Construction", "Price Construction", "Instrument Construction", "Approach Construction", "Location Construction", and "Field Construction", except the activation of the obtaining actor and object, the aim, price, instrument, approach, location, and field of the obtaining action is also activated, respectively, each of which has a typical expression in construction construal, for example, the propositional phrases "for…, with/for…, with…, by/via…, at/in…", and "in…"

are used. The action objects of the "Field Constructions" are usually some abstract concept, such as honor and fortune. The "Exchange Constructions" construe the concept of "two obtaining actors realize the aim of obtaining by exchange the objects", which could be further classified into two types. In the construction 1-8-1, the two obtaining actors have the same position and are expressed as double subjects in construction construe, linked by a conjunction "and". In the construction 1-8-2, the two obtaining actors do not have the same position or saliency, with one being the initiator of the exchanging action and be expressed as the subject of the construction and the other one not being the initiator of the exchange and be expressed as "with…" propositional phrase in construction construal.

(2) The object-change category of obtaining constructions

This category of constructions not only emphasize the object of the obtaining actions, but also overtly expresses the object-change caused by the obtaining action; both the action conceptual structure and the causing to change conceptual structure in the cognitive event frame are activated. The object-change obtaining constructions could be classified into 3 types (see construction 2-1 to 2-3 in Table 1). The "Original Owner Construction" emphasizes the original owner of the obtained object and the transfer of the object-possession from the original owner, which is expressed as the "from…" propositional phrase in construction construal. Similar to the "Original Owner Construction", the "Original Location Construction" also includes the overt expression of "from…" propositional phrase, but it is followed by certain location, such as a country, a town, and a store in this type of constructions, rather than by the original owner (person); this construction emphasizes not only the position-change of the object, but also the change of location of the obtained object. At last, since the sensory-motor practices of obtaining normally do not involve strong confrontation, the "Final Property Constructions" of obtaining generally emphasize the concept of the change of abstract properties (such as position and quality) of the obtained object, rather than the physical property of it.

The subject/theme of the above obtaining constructions are the obtainer, the present study also found a lot obtaining constructions that take the obtained object as the subject/theme (17/336, 5.06 %; see construction 4-1 to 4-6 in Table 1). The constructions taking the obtained object as the subject/theme express basically consistent conceptual content with those taking the obtainer as the subject/theme under the same title, but they emphasize different elements of the cognitive event frame.

Besides, as shown by the core obtaining cognitive event frame, the core conceptual content of the obtaining event certainly includes the concept of the obtaining action, and implies the concept of the change of the obtained object. The implied concept may not be overtly expressed in construction construal, and the present quantitative analysis proved this point: in the corpus of the obtaining constructions, only

56 constructions (14.29%) overtly expressed the concept of object-change and 245 constructions (72.92%) does not overly express this change concept.

Besides distributing in the two typical categories of obtaining constructions, i.e., the transitive category and the object-change category (271/336, 80.65%), the obtaining verbs also distribute in the "Made Obtain Construction", emphasizing the concept of "the obtainer made other people (the final owner) get or obtain an object (the obtained object)" (see construction 3-1-1 and 3-1-2 in Table 1). Both the "Made Obtain Construction" of the obtaining event and the "Final Direction/Possession Construction" of the giving event contain the concept of the result that "other people get or obtain the action object finally", and the differences are: the "Made Obtain Construction" emphasize the initiator of the obtaining action, who is both the direct obtainer and the indirect giver of the obtained object, with the final owner being the indirect obtainer of the object (expressed by "for…" propositional phrase); the initiator of the giving action in the "Final Direction/Possession Construction" is the direct giver of the object and the final owner is the direct receiver of the object. Please compare the following two sentences:

Carmen Direct obtainer/Indirect giver bought a dress (from Diana Original owner) for Mary Indirect obtainer/Final Owner. (Made Obtain Construction)

Carmen Direct giver gave a dress to Mary Direct obtainer/Final Owner. (Final Direction/Possession Construction)

4.3 Comparison between "Body—Brain—Form" Approach and Cognitive-Functional Approach

Theoretically, the main similarity of the two approaches is both of them pay great attention to the connection between the brain experiential knowledge network, the motor-sensory system and the language expression system, which coincide with the research perspective of the Embodied Language of Cognition (Glenberg, 1997; Barsalou, 1999; Anderson, 2003). The main difference of the two approaches lie in how to deal with the body (i.e., motor-sensory) aspect in the theoretical framework. According to the Cognitive Event Frame approach, conceptual meaning (in the brain) forms with grammatical structure representational relation through grammatical meaning, and grammatical meaning becomes the transition between such representative relation (Cheng 2006: 71), consequently, the form-meaning relation is turned into the relation between form (grammatical structure) and brain (conceptual meaning); this approach does not directly include the body (motor-sensory) aspect into the theoretical framework and could not directly describe the interaction of the motor-sensory system with the other two systems. The "Body—Brain—Form" Approach explicitly described the interaction and the dynamic connection between body, brain, and form, which is a more complete theoretical framework. The "Body—Brain—Form" Approach could more explicitly describe the dynamic connection between the body and the form, jointed by the brain, that is, specific "meaning" comes from the body (the sensory-motor practices), (which become a part of the experiential knowledge) stored in the brain, and embodied as certain language form (expression); at the same time, the processing of certain language expression needs to extract the "meaning" (related experiential knowledge) from the brain, which in turn actives the "meaning" (related sensory-motor experiences) from the body.

In application, this section adopted the Cognitive Event Frame approach to formulate the core conceptual content of the obtaining event, i.e., the part of the brain experiential knowledge network that all the obtaining practices involve and the processing of any obtaining construction would activate, and the elaborated conceptual content of the obtaining event, i.e., the whole experiential knowledge network that concludes all the elements and the complete processes of different sensory-motor practices of obtaining and the different paths of which would be activated by the processing of specific obtaining constructions. The present study shows that the Cognitive Event Frame approach could formulize the content of the experiential knowledge stored in the brain, which is economical in description and flexible in application. The present study used the "Body—Brain—Form" Approach to explain the construal mechanism of the obtaining construction, in specific, this section explicitly interpreted the three-dimensional construal processes from the source of the specific "meaning", i.e., the sensory-motor practices of obtaining, to specific obtaining constructions, with brain experiential knowledge network being the joint between the two aspects. The quantitative analysis of this section proved the rationality and accuracy of this explanation system in predicating the usage distribution of different obtaining constructions. Since the Cognitive Event Frame approach implies the connection of the sensory-motor system with the experiential knowledge brain network and the language expression system, it also could efficiently predicate the usage distribution of different constructions.

Chapter Five The "Conceptual Frame" Analysis to Physical Contact Event and Its Expressions

——————————————————————

5.1 Physical Contact Event

The word *event* was originally borrowed from the Middle French word *event* and from the Latin word *eventus* which means "occurrence, issue". Later, it acquires more usages. (Zhang, 2008).

In *Advanced Learner's English Dictionary* 10th by Oxford University Press, the word *event* is defined as:

1. a thing that happens, especially something important: *In the light of later event the decision was proved right.*

2. a planned public or social occasion: *a fund-raising event* ◇*the social event of the year.*

3. one of the races or competitions in a sports programme: *The 800 meters is the fourth event of the afternoon.* ------see also FIELD EVENT, TRACK EVENT

On the website: http://en.wikipedia.org/wiki/Wiki/_Event, there is such definition: "in the Unified Modeling Language, an event is a noticeable occurrence at a particular point in time. Events can, but not necessarily, cause state transitions from one state to another in state machines represented by state machine diagrams. ..."

Talmy (1991, 2000a, 2000b) claims that "a set of conceptual elements and relations that...are evoked together or co-evoke each other can be said to lie within or constitute an event-frame". Levin and Rappaport Hovav (1999) states "a verb lexicalizes a set of properties which are temporally anchored and a happening in the world with this set of properties is considered to be an event"

Based on the above definitions, the term *event* in our study is "an occurrence, a thing that happens or takes place at a particular point in space-time, which can, but not necessarily, cause state transitions from one state to another."

According to Cheng's viewpoint, the experience of each event would form a schema in the human brain, that is, the relational network of the process of certain event in the conceptual meaning system (These viewpoints of Cheng are concluded by the writer from her discussion with Cheng). In Cognitive-

Functional Approach (Cheng, 2002, 2005, 2006), the conceptual content (conceptual meaning) of an event is formulated as the conceptual frame of the event.

The conceptual content of physical contact event includes: "The action of the actor, through the controlled instrument (outer instrument or body parts of oneself), physically contact the object of the action, which would probably cause some change in the object in location, possession or property". Location, possession and property are all generalized as 'final'. The physical contact event can be illustrated by the following chart (These viewpoints are concluded by the writer from her discussion with Cheng and from the lecture of Cheng):

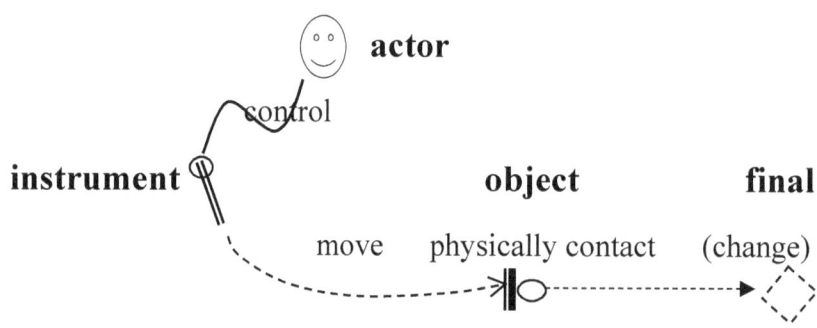

Chart1: Physical Contact Event

In this chart, the bold words: *actor, instrument, object,* and *final* indicate the participants of physical contact event; *control, move, physically contact* and *change* indicate the process of the event; the bracketed *change* indicates that the causing of change by the action is probable but not necessary.

As physical contact event is a principal part of human experiences which is vitally interrelated with human lives, various patterns of actions are involved in this kind of event. This variety is embodied in the linguistic expression system as different clauses, each of which both shares the general conceptual content of physical contact event and has the specific conceptual meaning of its own. The various clauses which share the conceptual content of physical contact event and have different sentence structures are called physical contact variants. The relationship between these variants is that of alternation.

The verbs that express the meaning of physical contact actions are physical contact verbs. The meaning of each physical contact verb bears certain correspondence to some sentence structures (variants) which represent specific action patterns. Then the meaning of verb and that of sentence structures impose restrictions on the entry of that verb into certain sentence structures.

5.2 The Corpus of Physical Contact Verbs and Constructions

In this thesis, physical contact verbs are mainly selected from the 18th (Verbs of Contact by Impact), the

19th (Poke verbs), and the 20th (Verbs of Contact: Touch Verbs) classes of verbs in Levin's book: *English Verb Classes and Alternations: A preliminary Investigation* (1993:148-156). They are:

Verb classes	18. Verbs of contact by impact
18.1 Hit verbs	hit, beat, strike, knock, bang, pound, smash (where no effect implicated), bump, drum, rap, tap, lash, slap, smack, kick, batter, hammer
18.2 Swat verbs	bite, claw, scratch, peck, stab, punch, swat
18.3 Spank verbs	belt, strap, cane, cosh, whip, knife, brain, conk
18.4Non-Agentive verbs	ram, slam, brush
	19. Poke verbs
	dig, pierce, poke, prick
	20. Verbs of contact: Touch verb
	touch, kiss, lick, pat, pinch, sting, tickle

Table1: Physical Contact Verbs

These three classes of verbs are all studied under the title of 'physical contact verbs' in a broad sense in this thesis because of the interrelatedness of the meaning of these verbs. For example, the 18th class: Verbs of Contact by Impact and the 19th class: Verbs of Contact: Touch Verbs in Levin's classification are all concerned with the action of contact. The strength of the actions expressed by Verbs of Contact by Impact range from very strong which can cause changes in the objects to very weak which could not cause change. Touch Verbs usually express the actions performed with little strength, which seldomly cause change. So these two classes of verbs are actually in a continuum in terms of the action strength they expressed. For example:

a. Somebody hit him a ball.

(http://books.google.com.hk/books?id=sEf2ai4XJ0sC&pg=PA142&lpg=PA142&dq=%22somebody+hit+him+a+ball%22&source=bl&ots=__n3jRakiL&sig=wPjEzauAuICWyaYhFB1ndZXdpKY&hl=zh-CN&ei=hcy0Tf3uDo-avgPf3P2HBw&sa=X&oi=book_result&ct=result&resnum=1&ved=0CBkQ6AEwAA#v=onepage&q=%22somebody%20hit%20him%20a%20ball%22&f=false)

*b. I rap him a ball. (T/?/F _/ /3)

*c. I touched him a ball.

Example a comes from the webpage of the novel *Safe by a mile* written by the native English writer

Charlie Metro, Thomas L. Altherr. Example b and c can not be found in any native English book or webpage and based on the judgments of native English speakers such usages are incorrect and unacceptable. *Hit* and *rap* both belong to the 18th class in Levin's classification, and *touch* belongs to the 19th class. However, both *rap* and *touch* express actions with weak power which can not cause possession change in the object. Besides, the 19th class: Poke verbs and most of the members of the 18.2th class: Swat verbs (*bite, claw, scratch, peck, stab*) all have the meaning of "bringing a pointed object into contact with a surface and, in some instances, puncturing the surface." So, these three classes of verbs are all studied under the title of 'physical contact verbs' in this thesis

The research method applied in this thesis is mainly that of 'data-driven', and the study would be unfolded as the works of corpus collection, classification and analysis are conducted.

The corpus collection work is carried out through the following procedures:

(1) To collect sentences patterns (variants) of each physical contact verb: some of them are taken from *A Dictionary of Current English Usage* (Zhang, 2003) and other dictionaries edited by native English speakers (marked D); some of them are searched and selected from English corpora, such as FrameNet and BNC (British National Corpus) (marked C); and some of them are found in publications of native English speakers (marked W) (see Appendix1: Corpus of Physical Contact Variants).

(2) To exhaust sentence patterns(variants) of every physical contact verb: to get a list of all the variants that physical contact verbs can enter from the sentence patterns collected in procedure (1), and then to repeat procedure (1) to find for each verb all the variants on the list.

(3) To supplement the inaccessible sentences patterns for some verbs: some sentence patterns can not be found for some verbs from the first two procedures, so they are made by the writer and the native English speakers are turned to to testify the correctness and acceptability of these sentences according to their language intuition and linguistic knowledge. The sentences that most native English speakers (the writer turns to 9 native English speakers altogether) regarded as correct and acceptable are taken as the variants of that verb; while the ones most of them regarded as incorrect or unacceptable are taken as the variants which that verb can not enter.

After these procedures, all variants for each physical contact verb are collected and we can observe which variants each verb can enter (see appendix2: Matrix of Physical Contact verbs).

5.3 Conceptual Content of Physical Contact Event

Event here means the relational network of the very event in the conceptual system, which is formulated as conceptual frame in Cognitive-Functional Approach (Cheng, 2002, 2005, 2006). The conceptual content of physical contact event includes: "The action of the actor, through the controlled instrument (outer instrument or body parts of oneself), physically contacts the object of the action, which would probably cause some changes in the object in location, possession or property". Location, possession and property are all generalized as "final".

In real world, three substances can be seen in physical contact event: the actor, the instrument, and the object, and at the same time the action, the movement and the possible changes can be observed. The action of physical contact is regarded as the confrontation of power between antitrope and antagonist, which can cause various changes in the objects. The conceptual meanings of confrontation and change are equivalent to Talmy (1991, 2000a, 2000b)'s Force-dynamics schema concerning the interaction between antitrope and antagonist. And in terms of the conceptual domain, the changes of object in location, possession and property can be specialized. Please compare:

Ted kicked the ball <u>into the net</u>.   [final location]

(www.docstoc.com/docs/20809332/English-Grammar-A-University-Course)

He kicked <u>her</u> a ball.   [final possession]

(http://www.lintroduction.com/Article_Show.asp?ArticleID=181)

He kicked her <u>black and blue</u>.   [final property]

(http://query.nytimes.com/gst/abstract.html?res=F40A11F63B59107B93C1A91783D85F448784F9)

These three kinds of changes are marked location, possession and property respectively. They are all 'final'. The shared conceptual content of the physical contact event, which connects with the perceptual and locomotor system, can be represented in this conceptual frame:

Actor	+ Physical contact action +Instrument +Object
Causer	+ Cause +Patient +Final

Here the actor coincides with the causer, and the object coincides with the patient.

Based on Cognitive-Functional Approach, verb meaning is one part of event meaning, and verb is one part of the clause. For instance, the verb *hit* can only express "the action in which the actor use certain instrument to hit something"; while the event meaning not only includes the verb meaning, but also implies the meaning of "the possible changes following the physical contact action". So the conceptual meaning of change is not a necessary result of physical contact event, but only the possible result. For the generality and economy of theoretical formulization, it is necessary to regard the various changes as outsides the specific action, but not the different meanings expressed by different verbs (Parts of the contents of this section come from the conclusion made by the writer from her discussion with Cheng).

5.4 Conception Meanings of Physical Contact Constructions

The conceptual frame in 3.2 formulates the conceptual content of physical contact event, which is shared by all the physical contact variants. On one hand such conceptual content connects with the perceptual and locomotor system, and on the other hand it can be construed as various variants. The conceptual meanings of physical contact variants are formulated as the elaboration of the generalized physical contact conceptual frame.

There are various variants representing the physical contact event, and such variety is firstly manifested in different topics. Theoretically all participants of the event can become the topic, and three kinds of topics are found in the linguistic expression of physical contact event. They are: actor, instrument and object. For example:

Tom kicked the ball into the net.   [actor]

(http://www.inclusive.org.nz/throughdifferenteyes/exemplars/tom-gets-play/x-learning-stories/story2)

The stick hit the fence.   [instrument]

(http://verbs.colorado.edu/verb-index/vn/hit-18.1.php)

Some glass smash in the other room.   [object]

(http://www.online-literature.com/wellshg/2867/)

Among the physical contact clauses, the actor-topiced ones are the most commom. Generally, the actor would be the topic when the clause is in active voice, while the instrument or the object would become the topic in the absence of an actor in a clause. This thesis mainly focuses on actor-topiced clauses.

The actor-topiced clauses can be construed as thirteen physical contact variants, and these thirteen alternaitons can be grouped into three classes according to the different perspectives. They are: the class of transitive action variants, the class of change in object variants, and the class of change in instrument variants. The elaborated conceptual frame concerning these thirteen variants is formulated as:

Actor + Physical contact action +Instrument + [Object + Part]
(Causer+Cause   + [Patient   + [Goal/Final direction and location /Resistance]/[Final direction/Final possession]/[Final property$_1$/final property$_2$]])
/(Causer+Cause   + [Object   +[Final direction or location/Resistance]])

Compared with the generalized conceptual frame, the elaborated one includes the "part", and the 'final' is elaborated as the final location, final possession and final property. Moreover, the causative conceptual structure expressing the movement of instrument is elaborated. According to the viewpoints of Cheng, as a relational network, the activation of different paths in the conceptual frame would be embodied as different grammatical structures, and the activation of the path is represented as the activation of certain semantic components, such as the participants. (These viewpoints of Cheng are concluded by the writer from her discussion with Cheng) In the following part, the activated components of each variant would be discussed respectively.

5.4.1 The Class of Transitive Action Constructions

This class of variants emphasize the state in which "the physical contact action involves the object", while the conceptual content of change in object is neglected. In conceptual frame, only the action conceptual structure is activated, and the causative conceptual structure is inactivated (In the following frame the bold parts mark the possibly activated components).

> **Actor + Physical contact action +Instrument + [Object + Part]**
> (Causer+Cause   + [Patient   + [Goal/Final direction and location /Resistance]
> /[Final direction/Final possession]/[Final property1/final property2]])
> /(Causer+Cause   + [Object   + [Final direction or location/Resistance]])

The class of transitive action variants can be divided into three subgroups, and they are transitive action alteration, instrument alteration and part variant, all of which exclude the conceptual meaning of change in object. For example:

Tom hit the ball.   [transitive action variant]
(http://www.iscribe.org/english/verb.html)

You hit the ball <u>with a club</u>.   [instrument variant]
(http://quantumminigolf.sourceforge.net/)

He hit a man <u>on the head</u>   [part variant]
(http://www.pressherald.com/archive/jury-gorham-officer-used-excessive-force_2009-03-25.html)

(1) Transitive Action Variant

Generally, the instrument participant would not be activated in transitive action alteration, but when the verbs (such as *whip* and *belt*) which simultaneously express action and instrument enter this variant the instrument would be activated. In this thesis, we call those verbs as *whip* and *belt* compound verb. We can compare:

a. He struck the house.

(myth.isgreat.org/thor-legend-myth.htm)

b. He whipped the horse.

(http://www.bukisa.com/articles/429405_his-friends-often-advised-him-to-say-good-bye-to-this-bad-habit)

The instrument in clause a would not be activated and represented, while in clause b both the instrument *whip* and the action of *whip* are activated. The activated components in the action conceptual structure include:

Transitive Action Alteration: *He whipped the horse.*

> **Actor** he + **Physical contact action** + (**Instrument** whip) + [**Object** horse + Part]
>
> ……

Here the action and the instrument are represented compoundedly by the verb *whip*.

(2) Instrument Variant

The instrument variant doesn't activate causative conceptual structure. Body-part of the object is also not activated. The instrument is the obligatorily activated part which is represented as *with* prepositional phrase, for wxample:

Instrument Alteration (1): *He hit the horse with club.*

> **Actor** he + **Physical contact action** hit + (**Instrument** club) + [**Object** horse + Part]
>
> ……

Though the activated components in instrumental variant are the same as these in transitive action alteration expressed by compound verb (such as *whip* and *belt* which simultaneously express action and instrument), the action and instrument in instrumental variant are represented as verb and *with* prepositional phrase respectively. Of course, the instrument variant also promises the blended representational relation of action and instrument, for example:

Instrument Alteration (2): *He whipped the horse with a long leather whip.*

> **Actor** he + **Physical contact action** + (**Instrument** a long leather whip) + [**Object** horse + Part]
>
> ……

Here the instrument participant is represented as *with* prepositional phrase, and at the same time instrument blends with the physical contact action as the verb *whip*. According to the economical principle, when a participant has two different representations simultaneously there must be certain kinds of semantic metonymy between them, or the clause would be regarded as improper by the native speakers. We can compare:

a. *Prince Ivan whipped the horse with his brand-new whip.*

(http://russian-crafts.com/tales/apple.html)

b. *?? He whipped the horse with a whip.*

(3) Part Variant

In part variant, instrument is an optional component, while the object must be activated and represented as the prepositional phrase in the end of the clause.

Part Variant: *He hit the all on the red spot.*

> **Actor** he + **Physical contact action** hit + (Instrument) + [**Object** ball + **Part** red spot]
>
> ……

5.4.2 The Class of Change in Object Constructions

The variants in this class share a common character that the object is salient in the variants and the change in the object is overtly represented. So in conceptual frame, the causative conceptual structure representing change in object must be activated.

The physical contact action may cause various changes in the object, which in terms of conceptual domain can be classified into three types: change in location, possession, and property. In the mental operation of physical contact event, only one kind of change would be activated, for example:

I kicked the ball into the net.   [final location]

(http://www.inclusive.org.nz/throughdifferenteyes/exemplars/tom-gets-play/x-learning-stories/story2)

She kicked him a ball.   [final possession]

(http://clresearch.blog.163.com/blog/static/382793902007111310261214/)

The police kicked him black and blue.   [final property]

(www.broccias.net/research/BrocciasRevECT-5.pdf)

Here, choice would be made from these three conceptual domains (in the conceptual frame it is marked by "/"). The mental operation of change in object variants only activates action conceptual structure and the first causative structure in conceptual frame. The 'object part' in the action structure is not activated. (In the following frame the bold parts mark the possibly activated components)

> **Actor** + **Physical contact action** +**Instrument** + [**Object** + Part]
>
> **(Causer+Cause** + [**Patient** + [**Goal/Final direction and location**
>
> **/Resistance**] /[**Final direction/Final possession**]/[**Final property1/final property2**]])
>
> /(Causer+Cause + [Object+ [Final direction or location/Resistance]])

According to conceptual domain, variants are classified into three kinds, and within each domain there are different variants.

(1) Location Domain

The variants representing change in location include goal variant, final location (and direction) variant, and resist variant, for example:

He kicked the ball at me. [goal variant]

(http://armorgames.com/community/thread/3606525/the-way-of-moderation-for-great-justice-page-507/page/191)

Tom kicked the ball into the net. [final direction and location variant]

(http://www.inclusive.org.nz/throughdifferenteyes/exemplars/tom-gets-play/x-learning-stories/story2)

I kicked the ball against the fence. [resist variant]

(http://www.theharvardadvocate.com/content/should-i-bring-flowers)

The goal variant represents the assumed goal of the moving path of the object, i.e., the mental aiming of the goal; the final direction and location variant represents the moving process (final direction) and ending position (final location) of the object; and the resist variant represents the confrontation of the power between the object and the final location entity. The goal variant, final location (and direction) variant, and resist variant are differentiated within the location domain, but only one of them is activated in the mental operation of a physical contact event, for example:

Final Direction and Location Variant: *Robert kicked the ball into the net.*

> **Actor** + **Physical contact action** +**Instrument** + [**Object** + Part]
>
> **(Causer+Cause** + [**Patient** + [Goal/**Final direction and location** /Resistance]/[Final
>
> direction/Final possession]/[Final property1/final property2]])
>
> /(Causer+Cause + [Object+ [Final direction or location/Resistance]])

Here only the 'final direction and location' is activated.

(2) Possession Domain

Within possession domain, mainly there are two kinds of variants. They are final direction variant and final possession variant, and only one of them would be activated in the mental operation.

He kicked the ball <u>to her</u>.   [final direction variant]

(http://www.english-for-students.com/Prepositions-1.html)

He kicked <u>her</u> a ball.   [final possession variant]

(http://www.lintroduction.com/Article_Show.asp?ArticleID=181)

The conceptual meanings of these two kinds of variants are different. Final direction variant emphasizes the direction of the change in possession, while final possession variant emphasizes the ending of the change and the acquisition of the object by the final possessor. For example:

Final Possession Variant: *John kicked <u>her</u> a ball.*

> **Actor** + **Physical contact action** +**Instrument** + [**Object** + Part]
>
> **(Causer+Cause**   + [**Patient**   + [Goal/Final direction and location /Resistance]/[Final direction/**Final possession**]/[Final property1/final property2]])
>
> /(Causer+Cause   + [Object   + [Final direction or location/Resistance]])

Besides, final direction variants in possession domain and location domain are of the same nature, and the only difference lies in the entity of the final. Please compare:

a. He kicked the ball to her.   [final direction variant- possession]

(http://www.english-for-students.com/Prepositions-1.html)

b. He kicked the ball to the net.   [final direction variant- location]

(http://www.fanfiction.net/s/88484/1/Tug_of_War_Basketball_and_Soccer)

The final of clause a is *her* which belongs to possession domain, while the final of clause b is *net* which belongs to location domain.

(3) Property Domain

Property change in object caused by physical contact action can be represented by two kinds of variants:

They beat him unconsciously. (Zhang, 2003)   [Final property variant1]

I'd smash his head into little pieces.   [Final property variant2]

(http://www.77ren.cn/viewthread.php?tid=636&page=1)

Final property variant1 use adjective or adverb to represent the final property, and final property variant2 use propositional phrase to represent the final property. In mental operation only one kind of variant would be activated, for example:

Final Property Variant1- Adjective]: *She beat him black and blue.*

> **Actor + Physical contact action +Instrument + [Object + Part]**
>
> **(Causer+Cause** + [**Patient** + [Goal/Final direction and location /Resistance]/[Final direction/Final possession]/[**Final property**1/final property2]])
>
> / (Causer+Cause + [Object+ [Final direction or location/Resistance]])

In conclusion, change the object variants all emphasize the object and the change in object caused by physical contact action. The highlighted objects are all represented as the noun phrases in the object position of the clause. The instruments are neglected, sometimes having no overt expression in the clause.

5.4.3 The Class of Change in Instrument Constructions

In this class the instrument is salient in the variants and the change in instrument is overtly represented. In the form-meaning representational relation, the emphasis of the instrument is the overt representation of the moving process and final location of the instrument, or the representation of the power opposition between the instrument and the final location entity. These two kinds of representations formed two variants in this class: final direction and location variant and resistance variant:

He struck his axe into the tree. [final direction and location variant]

(books.google.com.hk/books?isbn=0486256685...)

He smashed his fist against the door. [resistance variant]

(http://www.fanfiction.net/s/1232032/10/Last_Thing_I_Wanted)

In conceptual frame, change in instrument is mainly represented by the second causative conceptual structure. The object in this causative conceptual frame coincides with the instrument in the action structure, and its final (the final direction and location/resistance in the frame) coincides with the action object. In the mental operation process, both the action conceptual structure and the second causative structure are activated, with the first causative structure half activated, for example:

Instrument resistance variant: *He pouched his fist against the table.*

Actor + Physical contact action +Instrument + [Object + Part]		
(Causer+Cause	+ [Patient	+ [Goal/Final direction and location /Resistance]
/[Final direction/Final possession]/[Final property₁/final property₂]])		
/ (Causer+Cause	+ [Object	+ [Final direction or location/Resistance]])

Except the subject, one clause only emphasizes one participant which is represented as the noun phrase in the object position of the clause. The emphasized participant corresponds to the 'trajector' in Langacker's theory (1987, 1990, 1991). The components of object complement further illustrate the conceptual content of the participant which equals to Langacker's 'landmark'. It is observed that no matter it emphasizes the object or the instrument, there exist final direction and location and resistance in the landmark. Of course, there is difference between the landmark of the change in object variants and the change in instrument variants, i.e., the landmark object can be goal, but goal can not be the landmark of instrument. Cheng suggests that this difference in the landmark of object and instrument basically corresponds to the human experiences in the world. The instrument, which is controlled by the actor, can easily hit the object, so goal variant which emphasizes the "assumed goal of the object" does not belong to the class of change in instrument variants; while the arrival of the object at the goal position is much more difficult for its moving process is not directly controllable by the actor. The different experiences of people in the world are represented as different variants in English language.

5.5 The Relationship between Physical Contact Verbs and Their Constructions

As one part of physical contact event, physical contact action involves actor, instrument, and object. According to the definition of physical contact event in this thesis, the actions expressed by Verbs of Contact by Physical contact (the 18th class of verbs in Levin's classification) almost all belong to physical contact action.

In terms of body-parts, hand and foot are all involved in physical contact action. But the number of verbs representing the actions performed by hand is bigger than that performed by foot. There is only one foot-specific verb, *kick*; while the hand-specific verbs include *hit, strike, pound, bump, bang, beat, drum, rap, tap, slap, swab, smack, punch, smash, batter, stab, whip, belt, strap, cane, lash, knife, hammer*, and so on. The large amount of hand-specific verbs expressing richer and more refined conceptual meaning manifests that most of physical contact actions must be performed by hands in human experiences. In terms of semiotic relationship, the hand-specific verbs bear more complicated relationship with their variants than foot-specific verbs.

In terms of semiotic relations, some physical contact verbs, as well as many other classes of verbs (such as *butter, pocket, fence*), bear compound representational relations, i.e., one verb represent "action" and a participant of that action simultaneously. This kind of physical contact verbs can be further grouped under two heads, for example:

Our teacher <u>belted</u> the boy.   [action+ instrument]

(http://answers.yahoo.com/question/index?qid=20101026050941AAQLQqA)

Policeman reported the man was <u>drumming</u>.   [action +final location]

(http://articles.ocregister.com/keyword/drummer)

The verb *belt,* expressing 'to belt with a belt', represents both the action of belt and the instrument of the action. Such verbs are called 'instrumental verbs'. The verb *drum,* expressing 'to drum the object', represents both the action and the object. Such verbs are called 'object verb'. Besides, the meaning of 'to beat as beating a drum' can also be derived from the English verb *drum,* for example:

He drummed the door.   [action + action pattern]

(http://www.foroyaa.gm/modules/news/article.php?storyid=864)

Here drum is a verb expressing specific action pattern, and no longer a final location verb.

Most of the 18.3[th] class of verbs (such as *lash, belt, strap, cane, cosh, knife* and *conk*) in Levin's classification can be grouped into instrumental verbs. Besides, *lash* in the 18.1[th] class should also be classified as instrumental verbs. And the class of object verb has only one member: *drum.*

Most of the physical contact verbs do not bear compound representational relations. Except the conceptual content of "physical contact", different physical contact verbs have different semantic components, including 'physical contact strength' and 'physical contact effect'. The strength of action expressed by verb *rap, hit, knock, pound, smash, and batter* range from the weakest to the strongest. Verbs representing actions performed with strong power such as *knock, smash, and batter* and verbs expressing repeated action of physical contact such as *beat* have the tendency of 'physical contact effect' which means the action would probably destroy the object.

5.5.1 Transitive Action Constructions

In this thesis, mainly three subclasses of physical contact variants are classified: the transitive action variants, change in object variants, and change in instrument variants. Through the systematic analysis of physical contact verbs, it is found that the productivity of the variants in these three subclasses is different and the restrictive conditions to the verbs are different. The variants in the transitive action subclass are highly productive with most of the physical contact verbs being able to enter the variants in this subclass.

Though most of the physical contact verbs can enter instrument variant, the "instrumental verbs" has their own semantic restrictions, for example:

Tom whipped the kids with a long leather whip.

?? Tom whipped the kids with whip.

The verb *whip* expresses both the action of 'whip' and the instrument of 'whip'.

Because the verb compoundly represents action and instrument, if there appears instrumental expression in the grammatical structure, the expression must be different from the word *whip*. Based on the economic principle of expression, the metonymic representation of the instrument participant is common. In the above example, there exists 'part- whole' metonymic semantic relation between *long leather whip* and *whip*.

Though the verb drum can be compound representational verb, in instrument variant the lexical item expressing instrument can not be the same as the verb, for the 'object verb' *drum* compoundly expresses the action and the object.

5.5.2 Change in Object Constructions

The physical contact action acts on and even causes some changes in the object. The change may be location, possession or property change. With regard to physical contact verbs, the number of verbs entering property variants is the largest, and number of verbs entering possession variants is the smallest, with the number of verbs entering location variant in the middle. Such relation between verb and variant shows that the physical contact verbs are mainly a kind of causative verb which causes change in the property.

(1) Property Change

The physical contact verbs with "physical contact effect" meaning component (such as *smack, punch, smash*, and *batter*) obvious include the meaning of property change, so native English speakers have no controversy in their entry into property change variants. Besides, the semantic component "physical contact strength" also has some influence on the verb-variant relation. The verb expressing action performed with strong power can more easily enter into the property change variants, for example:

※ *Tom rapped her to death.*

?? Tom hit her to death.

He struck her to death.

(books.google.com.hk/books?id=TT09AAAAYAAJ...)

I'll beat her to death.

(http://www.nairaland.com/nigeria/topic-16431.0.html)

A housewife battered her to death.

(http://www.facebook.com/group.php?gid=148570355596)

The strength of the verb *rap* is weak; while that of *hit* and *strike* are strong; the strength of *batter* is big enough to influence the object; *beat* include the meaning of "repeated action", so *the action expressed by strike, batter* and *beat* are more likely to cause property change in object. As a consequence, these powerful and influential verbs can enter the property change variants, while rap has no such access. And most native English speakers believe *hit* can't be enter this variant.

Most of the physical contact verbs can enter both property variant1 and property variant2. The property of the former is expressed by adjective or adverb, and that of the latter is expressed by *to* propositional phrase. The verb-variant relations in these two kinds of variants are different. Some of the 'instrument verbs' can not enter property variant1, such as *strap, cane, cosh, knife, conk*, and *lash*; while the frequently used *hammer, whip, belt* can enter this variant.

(2) Location Change

The physical contact verbs that have access to enter location change variants expressing the location change in the object caused by physical contact action. Based on the human experience in the world, the actions with weak strength are hard to cause movement of the object, such as *rap*. The verbs emphasizing property changes are also difficult to overtly express location change, such as *batter* and *stab*. For the economy of expression, the "instrument verbs" (such as *belt, strap, cane, cosh, knife,* and *conk*) which overtly express the "action performed through instrument" do not enter final direction and location variant which represent the movement of the object.

Compared with the entry of physical contact verbs in final direction and location variants, the number of verbs entering resistance variants is smaller. The semantic conditions controlling its entry are hard to define, but some verbs are known not to enter this variant. They are: the verb expressing actions performed with weak strength, such as *rap, tap,* and *slap;* the verb *batter* which includes "physical contact effect" meaning; and most of the instrument verb.

The number of physical contact verbs entering goal variant is smaller than these entering final direction and location variants and resistance variants, and its certain members are *kick* and *whip.*

(3) Possession Change

In English language, it is not used to express physical contact event in terms of possession change variant. In this study, only *kick* and *hit* enter this variant.

5.5.3 Change in Instrument Constructions

As is shown in the conceptual frame, the salient participant in physical contact event is optional. It may be object or instrument of the action. The variants further manifest whether the participants or the resistance of strength or the change by the physical contact is emphasized. The variants emphasizing instrument are smpler than that emphasizing object, and it only express location change and confrontation of power after physical contact. Please compare:

Shetler struck the ball into the net.   [location change-object]

(http://www.iowamennonite.org/category/athletics/page/25/)

David struck the axe into the tree.   [location change-instrument]

(http://www.archive.org/stream/textbookofchurch02kurt/textbookofchurch02kurt_djvu.txt)

He kicked the ball against the fence.   [resistance-object]

(http://www.netmums.com/coffeehouse/general-coffeehouse-chat-514/wine-bar-494/460477-footballs-over-fence.html)

Hsrry kicked his leg against the table   [resistance-instrument]

(http://www.fanfiction.net/s/3265892/9/Silver_Wolf)

Not all physical contact verbs enter change in instrument variants. Through the study of the data in this thesis, it is found that the compound representational verbs normally do not enter this class of variants.

The non-compound representational verbs normally enter the resistance variant of instrument change, but seldom enter the final direction and location variant with the only exception of *strike*.

5.6 Revisions to Levin's Classification of Physical Contact Verbs

Based on the conceptual meanings of physical contact verbs and their distribution in variants, the following revisions can be made to Levin's classification of physical contact verbs.

(1) The distribution of most of the verbs in 18.2 (*bite, claw, scratch, peck, stab, punch, swat*) are similar to that of Poke verbs. They normally do not enter resist variant which expresses the confrontation of power between the two same objects, for example:

Most people today, "hit stick against stick"

(http://www.martialartsplanet.com/forums/showthread.php?t=63055)

He bites one stick against another.

They normally do not enter final possession variant, for example:

A big boy hits a ball to him.

(http://www.amazon.com/Rookie-Year-Thomas-Ian-Nicholas/product-reviews/B0007LLPXI?pageNumber=4)

He hits him a ball.

(http://www.amazon.com/Sandlot-Tom-Guiry/product-reviews/B00005RT3N?pageNumber=6)

He pokes a ball to him.

He pokes him a ball.

Besides, the final direction variant with a *through* proposition which expresses 'puncturing the surface' and the instrument alteration with a *with* proposition are characteristic of these verbs. Moreover, they all involve the conceptual content of 'bringing a pointed object into contact with a surface and, in some instances, puncturing the surface'. So it is more proper to classify Swat Verbs of 18.2 in Levin's classification into Poke verbs.

(2) The verb *punch* and *swat* are more similar to Hit verbs than Swat verbs in their entry in alternaitons. These two verbs can enter almost all the variants in which Hit verbs enter, including the resist variant and the final possession variant in which other Swat verbs seldom appear. They also share the same conceptual content of Hit verbs: 'moving one entity in order to bring it into contact with another entity'. So it is more proper to put *punch* and *swat* into class18.1: Impact verbs.

Besides, the title of 18.2, Swat verbs, is not proper since the verb *swat* is not the typical verb of this subclass in terms of conceptual content and distribution in variants.

(3) The verb *lash* in 18.1 expresses 'to lash with a lash' which represents compoundly the action of lash and the instrument of the action. It can be classified as 'instrumental verbs' whose memberships are mainly Spank verbs. So, it is more proper to put *lash* into 18.3: Spank verbs.

After these revisions, a new classification of physical contact verbs can be made:

Verb types	1. Verbs of contact by impact
1.1 Hit verbs	hit, beat, strike, knock, bang, pound, smash (where no effect implicated), bump, drum, rap, tap, slap, smack, kick, batter, hammer, **punch, swat**
1.2 Spank verbs	belt, strap, cane, cosh, whip, knife, brain, conk, **lash**

1.3 Non-Agentive verbs	ram, slam, brush
	2. Poke verbs
	dig, pierce, poke, prick, **bite, claw, scratch, peck, stab**
	3. Verbs of contact: Touch verb
	touch, kiss, lick, pat, pinch, sting, tickle

Table2 Classification of Physical Contact Verbs by Conceptual Frame

5.7 Comparison between Cognitive-Functional Approach and Construction Grammar

5.7.1 The Similarities between the Two Approaches

Firstly, these two approaches both center on meaning and are interpretational mechanisms of meaning. The Cognitive-Functional Approach (Cheng, 2002, 2005, 2006) formulates the conceptual meanings of sentences by conceptual frames, while Construction Grammar (1995, 2010) holds that each construction has its specific meaning which provides arguments directly.

(Jackondoff, 1990, 2002, 2007), Cognitive Semantics (Talmy, 1991; 2000a; 2000b), Construction Grammar (Goldberg, 1995, 2010), Cognitive Grammar (Langacker, 1987, 1990, 1991), have

Secondly, these two approaches both take Cognitive Linguistics as their theoretical background and both get enlightened by Frame Semantics of Fillmore (1968, 1982, 1997), Cognitive Semantics of Langacker (1987, 1990, 1991), Semantic Structure of Jackondoff (1990, 2002, 2007), metaphorical and prototype theories and Force Dynamics theory of Talmy (1991; 2000a; 2000b).

Thirdly, these two approaches both emphasize the relatedness of meaning with human experience. Conceptual frame is interconnected with the perceptual locomotor system and linguistic expression; and construction connects with the dynamic situations based on human experiences

Fourthly, these two models both emphasize the integration of verb meaning with structure meaning. Cognitive-Functional Approach holds that one word can activate a conceptual frame, and the conceptual frame of words and clause are interconnected. Construction Grammar emphasizes the fusion of participant roles of verbs and the construction roles.

5.7.2 The Differences between the Two Approaches

Firstly, conceptual frame approach is a more open and comprehensive mechanism in meaning description. The conceptual domains are divided into location, possession and property domains; and according to three kinds of conceptual relations, spatio-temperal existence structure, active structure and causative structure are distinguished. They include various semantic types which can properly explain various sentence structures.

On the contrary, there are only five major argument constructions in Construction Grammar and they can only explain the meaning of the sentences which coincide with these five constructions in structure. This approach can not explain instrument variant, part variant, and final property variant2 which are reasonably analyzed and classified under Cognitive-Functional Approach.

Secondly, Cognitive-Functional Approach allows exquisite division of meaning. For example, the causative variants (change in object\instrument variant) are divided into final location variant, final possession variant, and final property variant. For example:

He hit the stick to the ground.   [final location]

(http://www.urch.com/forums/graduate-admissions/2049-your-essay-should-bring-you-reader-closer.html)

I hit a ball to him.   [final possession]

(http://www.facebook.com/note.php?note_id=171443540637&comments)

Watch Zack hit the door down.   [final property]

(http://gamerstrueparadise.wordpress.com/crisis-core-ffvii-psp/)

In turn, the final location is divided into goal variant, final direction and location variant, and resist variant according to the propositional phrases used to realize the conceptual meaning; the final possession is divided into final direction variant and final possession variant; the final property is also divided into two kinds according to the complement component used to realize the conceptual meaning. For example:

He calmly struck the ball at goal.   [goal variant]

(http://gamerstrueparadise.wordpress.com/crisis-core-ffvii-psp/)

Samia struck the ball into the net.   [final direction and location variant]

(http://www.eteamz.com/deanzaforce95blue/)

Butt struck the ball against wall.   [resist variant]

(http://origin-www.mfc.co.uk/page/matches/reports/0,,1~44161,00.html)

Russell struck a ball to John Oliver.   [final direction variant]

(http://www.nytimes.com/1860/07/20/news/door-sports-base-ball-excelsior-vs-atlantic-excelsiors-victorious-champion-club.html?pagewanted=all)

I struck <u>him a ball</u>. (Zhang 2003)　　　　　　　　[final possession variant]

He struck a tree <u>down</u>.　　　　　　　　　　　　[final property variant1]

(http://www.bulgariansearesorts.com/resorts/golden_sands/hotels/sofia_hotel_313)

Rhetoric and reality struck him <u>into a mindless heap</u>　　[final property variant2]

(s3.amazonaws.com/manybooksfb/coopermother092012fb2.fb2)

Besides, the changes in object and instrument are distinguished. For example:

He struck the <u>stick</u> against the rock.　　　　　　[resist: change in the instrument]

(http://www.politedissent.com/index.php?s=jane+foster&submit=search)

Butt struck the <u>ball</u> against wall.　　　　　　　[resist: change in the object]

(http://origin-www.mfc.co.uk/page/matches/reports/0,,1~44161,00.html)

Moreover, the most significant of Cognitive-Functional Approach is the distinction of different topics in the expression of physical contact event (mainly actor, instrument, and object). For example:

He struck at the wall.　　　　　　　　　　　　　[actor]

(http://amy-from-mars.com/home/amyfrommarspage07.html)

The head of the stick strikes the center of the drum.　　　[instrument]

(http://forums.creativecow.net/archivethread/102/246604)

The ball strikes the stick.　　　　　　　　　　　[object]

(http://forums.iseekgolf.com/forums/14-rules-of-golf/topics/31459-perils-of-having-flag-attended-in-matchplay)

On the contrary, in Construction Grammar, each construction is defined as having a specific meaning, so the refined meaning distinction in the same structure can not be explained.

Thirdly, Cognitive-Functional Approach allows combinations of different conceptual meaning structures which can express various conceptual meaning, while Construction Grammar directly defines five kinds of constructions and the metaphorical extension of meaning is also based on the central meaning of these five constructions. Cognitive-Functional Approach has stronger productive and extensive ability.

Fourthly, a more proper explanation can be made to the meanings and classifications of physical contact verbs under Cognitive-Functional Approach. Through the mechanism of construction, the brief distinctions between Hit verbs and other subclasses, such as Spank verbs, Poke verbs, and Touch verb can be made; but the differences between Spank verbs and Poke verbs can not be shown. This is resolved by Cognitive-Fuctional Approach.

5.8 Summary of Chapter Five

The objective of this chapter is to discuss the semantic correspondence between physical contact verbs and their variants under Cognitive-Functional Approach (Cheng, 2002, 2005, 2006).

Levin did an extensive job in data collection and made classification of verbs according to their syntactic behavior. The constructions defined in Construction Grammar and the idea of extension in the meaning of the basic constructions do enlighten other studies in the field of form-meaning relation. But some problems in their theory and methodology may weaken her research, for instance, the incompleteness coarseness and fussiness of the definition of the meaning of certain verb classes and constructions, the improperness in the division of subgroups of verbs, and the failure in illustrating the detailed and specific meaning of each type of grammatical structures (variants). These problems indicate that more precise and effective models that can refine the classification and semantic analysis of physical contact verbs are called for.

In this part, the writer constructs conceptual frames to explore and theoretically formulate the conceptual content of the physical contact event which is shared by all the physical contact variants and the specific conceptual meaning of each kind of physical contact variant through which the semantic correspondence between physical contact verbs and their variants would be illustrated by the study of such form-meaning semiotic relation. And based on this, the contrast between Cognitive-Functional Approach and Construction Grammar can be drawn.

The conceptual content of physical contact event includes: 'The action of the actor, through the controlled instrument (outer instrument or body parts of oneself), physically contact the object of the action, which would probably cause some change in the object in location, possession or property'. The shared conceptual content of the physical contact event, which connects with the perceptual and locomotor system, can be represented in the following conceptual frame:

Actor + Physical contact action +Instrument +Object	
Causer + Cause	+Patient +Final

The physical contact variants are various, which are firstly manifested in different topics among which the actor-topiced variants are the main focus. The actor-topiced clause of physical contact event can be construed into thirteen variants, which are grouped into three classes according to different perspectives. The elaborated conceptual frame concerning these thirteen variants is formulated as:

> Actor + Physical contact action +Instrument + [Object + Part]
>
> (Causer+Cause + [Patient + [Goal/Final direction and location /Resistance]/[Final direction/Final possession]/[Final property1/final property2]])v
>
> /(Causer+Cause + [Object+[Final direction or location/Resistance]])

The three classes of actor-topiced physical contact variants are: the class of transitive action variants, the class of change in the object variants, the class of change in the instrument variants.

The class of transitive action variants emphasize the 'involvement of the object by the physical contact action', while the conceptual content of the change in the object is weakened. In its conceptual frame only the action conceptual structure is activated with the causative conceptual structure remaining inactivated (In the following conceptual frame the bold parts mark the possibly activated components).

> **Actor + Physical contact action +Instrument + [Object + Part]**
>
> (Causer+Cause + [Patient + [Goal/Final direction and location /Resistance] /[Final direction/Final possession]/[Final property1/final property2]])
>
> /(Causer+Cause + [Object + [Final direction or location/Resistance]])

This class of variants are divided into three subgroups, all of which exclude the conceptual meaning of change in object.

[The transitive action alteration]: *He whipped the horse.*

> **Actor** he + **Physical contact action** + (**Instrument** whip) + [**Object** horse + Part]
>
> ......

[Instrument alteration (1)]: *He hit the horse with club.*

> **Actor** he + **Physical contact action** hit + (**Instrument** club) + [**Object** horse + Part]
>
> ......

[Instrument alteration (2)]: *He whipped the horse with a long leather whip.*

> **Actor** he + **Physical contact action** + (**Instrument** a long leather whip) + [**Object** horse + Part]
>
> ......

[Part variant]: *He hit the ball on the red spot.*

> **Actor** he + **Physical contact action** hit + (Instrument) + [**Object** ball + **Part** red spot]
>
> ......

The cognitive operation of the changes in the object variants only activates action conceptual structure and the first causative structure in the frame. But the 'object part' in the action structure is not activated. (In the following frame the bold parts mark the possibly activated components)

> **Actor + Physical contact action +Instrument + [Object + Part]**
>
> **(Causer+Cause** + [**Patient** + [**Goal/Final direction and location /Resistance]**
>
> /[**Final direction/Final possession]/[Final property1/final property2]])**
>
> /(Causer+Cause + [Object + [Final direction or location/Resistance]])

Three kinds of variants can be distinguished in this class of variants according to conceptual domain: location domain, possession domain, and property domain (as is shown in the above conceptual frame).

In the conceptual frame, change in the instrument is mainly represented by the second causative conceptual structure. The object in this causative conceptual frame coincides with the instrument in the action structure, and its final (the [Final directionr and location/Resistance] in the frame) coincides with the action object. In the cognitive operation process, both the action conceptual structure and the second causative structure are activated, with the first causative structure being half activated, for example:

[instrument resistance variant]: *He pouched his fist against the table.*

> **Actor + Physical contact action +Instrument + [Object + Part]**
>
> (Causer+Cause + [Patient + [Goal/Final direction and location /Resistance]
>
> /[Final direction/Final possession]/[Final property1/final property2]])
>
> / (**Causer+Cause** + [**Object** + [Final direction or location/**Resistance**]])

Through the construction of conceptual frames, the general conceptual content of the physical contact event which is shared by all the physical contact variants and the specific conceptual meaning of each kind of physical contact variant are described and theoretically formulated. Thus the correspondence between physical contact verbs and their variants are clearly illustrated. It is found that the productivity of different variants in the three subclasses is different and the restrictive conditions to the verbs are different. The variants in the transitive action subclass are highly productive with most of the physical contact verbs being able to enter into the three kinds of variants in this subclass.

Though most of the physical contact verbs can enter into instrument variant, the 'instrumental verbs' have their own semantic restrictions. Based on the economic principle of expression, the metonymic representation of the instrument participant is common.

The physical contact action acts on and even causes some change (in location, possession or property) in the object. The number of physical contact verbs that can enter property variant is the largest, and that entering possession variant is the smallest. Most of the physical contact verbs can enter both property variant1 and property variant2. Some of the 'instrument verbs' seldom appear in property variant1, such as *strap, cane, cosh, knife, conk,* and *lash*; while the frequently used verbs *hammer, whip, belt* being able to enter this variant.

Based on the human experience in the outer world, the actions with weak strength are hard to cause movement of the object, such as *rap*. The verbs emphasizing property change are also difficult to overtly express location change, such as *batter* and *stab*. Due to the economy principle of expression, the 'instrument verbs' (such as *belt, strap, cane, cosh, knife, conk*) which overtly express the 'action by the instrument' don't enter into final direction and location variant which represent the movement of the object. Some verbs are known not to enter resistance variant. They are: the verb with weak strength, such as *rap, tap,* and *slap;* the verb batter which includes 'physical contact effect' meaning; and most of the instrument verb. The number of physical contact verbs entering goal variant is less than the other two, and its certain members are *kick* and *whip.*

In English language, it is not used to express physical contact event in terms of possession change variant. In this study, only *kick* and *hit* enter this variant.

Through the study of language data, it is found that the compound representational verbs normally don't enter change in the instrument variants. The non-compound representational verbs normally enter the resistance variant of instrument change, but seldom enter the final direction and location variant with the only exception of strike.

Based on the conceptual meanings of physical contact verbs and their distribution in the variants, revisions to Levin's classification of the physical contact verbs are made.

(1) The distribution of most of the verbs in 18.2 (*bite, claw, scratch, peck, stab, punch, swat*) are similar to that of the Poke verbs. They normally do not appear in the [resist variant] and the [final possession variant]. The [final direction variant] with a *through* proposition which expresses 'puncturing the surface' and the [instrument alteration] with a *with* proposition are characteristic of these verbs. Moreover, they all involve the conceptual content of 'bringing a pointed object into contact with a surface and, in some instances, puncturing the surface'. So it is more proper to classify the Swat Verbs of 18.2 into the class of Poke verbs.

(2) The verb *punch* and *swat* are more similar in distribution to Hit verbs of 18.1 than the Swat verbs of 18.2. The two verbs can distribute in almost all the variants of 18.1 verbs, including the [resist variant] and the [final possession variant] in which other 18.2 verbs seldom appear. They also share the same

conceptual content of Hit verbs. So it is more proper to put *punch* and *swat* into 18.1. Besides, they class title of 18.2, Swat verbs, is not proper since the verb *swat* isn't characteristic of this subclass in conceptual content and variant distribution.

(3) The verb *lash* in 18.1 expresses 'to lash with a lash' which represents compoundly the action of lash and the instrument of the action. It can be included as the class of 'instrumental verbs' which takes most of the Spank verbs of 18.3 as its members. So, it is more proper to put *lash* into 18.3.

Based on the above descriptions, the comparison between Cognitive-Functional Approach and Construction Grammar in their description of physical contact verbs is made. The similarities between these two models are: Firstly, they both center on meaning and are interpretational mechanisms of meaning. Secondly, these two models both take Cognitive linguistics as their theoretical background. Thirdly, these two models both emphasize the relatedness of meaning with human experience. Fourthly, these two models both emphasize the integration of verb meaning with structure meaning.

The differences between these two models are: Firstly, conceptual frame approach is a more open and comprehensive mechanism to describe meaning compared with Construction Grammar. Secondly, the Conceptual Frame approach allows exquisite division of meaning. While in Construction Grammar, each construction has a specific meaning and the refined meaning distinction in the same structure can't be explained. Thirdly, the Conceptual Frame approach allows combinations of different conceptual meaning structures which are forbidden in Construction Grammar. As a consequence, the Conceptual Frame approach bears much more productivity and extensibility. Fourthly, a more proper explanation can be made to the meanings and classifications of physical contact verbs by Conceptual Frame approach. Some of the problems in such work by Construction Grammar mechanism can be resolved by Conceptual Frame approach. Compared with Conceptual frame approach, there exist more limitations in Construction Grammar which restrict the fusion of verb meaning and structure meaning

So, it can be concluded that the objective of this thesis has been achieved, that is, to discuss the semantic correspondence between physical contact verbs and their variants through constructing conceptual frames to theoretically formulate the generally shared conceptual content of physical contact events and the specific conceptual meaning of each kind of physical contact variant. Some of the problems exist in Lexical semantics and Construction Grammar in their application to describe physical contact verbs, for instance, the incompleteness, coarseness and fussiness of the definition of the meaning of certain verb classes and constructions, the improperness in the division of subgroups of verbs, and the failure in illustrating the detailed and specific meaning of each type of grammatical structures (variants) are resolved by Cognitive-Functional Approach. At last, based on such discussion, comparisons are made between

Cognitive-Functional Approach and Construction Grammar in their application in describing physical contact verbs.

Chapter Six The "Conceptual Frame" Analysis to Delivery Event and Its Expressions

━━━◆ ◆▣ ◆✖ ◆◲ ◆▱━━━

6.1 Delivery Event and Related Corpus

The word "delivery" was borrowed from the Anglo-Norman French word "delivree". In the *Oxford Advanced Learner's English-Chinese Dictionary* (the 7th edition, 2009), the word delivery is defined as:

1. The action of delivering letters, parcels, or ordered goods: *allow up to 28 days for delivery.*

2. A regular or scheduled occasion for this: *there will be 15 deliveries a week.*

In 《现代汉语词典》第 7 版 (2016), The Chinese word "递送" is defined as: "送 (公文、信件等); 投递". The English term delivery in this study is "an action of transit by an actor, which usually can change an object's final location or possession." And the Chinese term "递送" shares the same conceptual meaning.

The conceptual content of delivery event includes: the actor; the delivery action of the object (an actor could move with the object or not); the change of the object in location, possession and state. There are three participants in the delivery event: "actor, object and final". The "final" here represents the final result of the object after the completion of the delivery action, which can be divided into final location, final possession and final state.

In this study, delivery verbs are mainly selected from the 11th (Verbs of Sending and Carrying) classes of verbs in Levin (1993)'s book: *English Verb Classes and Alternation*, which are:

11.1 Send Verbs: airmail, convey, deliver, dispatch, express, forward, hand, mail, pass, port, return, send, shift, ship, shunt, slip, smuggle, sneak, transfer, transport;

11.2 Slide Verbs: bounce, float, move, roll, slide;

11.3 Bring and Take: bring, take;

11.4 Carry Verbs: carry, drag, haul, heave, heft, hoist, kick, lug, pull, push, schlep, shove, tote, tow, tug;

11.5 Drive Verbs: barge, bus, cart, drive, ferry, fly, row, shuttle, truck, wheel, wire (money). These five verbs studied in this study are called "delivery verbs" because the meanings of these verbs are interrelated. For instance, the Send Verbs in Levin (1993)'s book are all related with causing an object to change location. Slide Verbs can be used as intransitive verbs of manner of motion. Bring and Take can be described as "verbs of continuous causation of accompanied motion in a deictically-specified direction". Carry Verbs are related to the causation of accompanied motion. Drive Verbs describe the causation of accompanied motion, typically by the vehicle or means.

This thesis mainly uses "data-driven" method, and the study is carried out with the collection, classification and analysis of corpus.

The procedures of corpus collection are as follows: (1) Collecting English variants of each delivery verb: some of them are selected from *A Dictionary of Current English Usage* (《现代英语用法词典》; Zhang, 2003) and other authoritative dictionaries; some of them are searched and selected from English corpora, such as COCA (Corpus of Contemporary American English); and some of them are found on the website, such as Google, Baidu and Youdao. For Chinese verbs: some of them are taken from *A Dictionary of Chinese Verb Usage* (《汉语动词用法词典》, Meng, 1999) ; some of them are searched and selected from Chinese corpora and internet, such as BBC (BLCU Corpus Center) and Baidu. (2) To exhaust the variants of every delivery verb: to obtain a data base of all variants that can be input by delivery verbs from the variants collected in procedure (1). After that, we can analyze all variants of each delivery verbs to find correspondence between delivery verbs and their variants.

6.2 Previous Studies on Delivery Verbs

The delivery verbs studied in this thesis are mainly selected from Levin's book *English Verb Classes and Alternations* (1993).

According to the assumption that a verb's syntactic behavior is largely determined by its meaning, and if class members share some meaning parts then they exhibit the same syntactic behavior.

Levin makes an analysis and a classification of alternations according to verb's properties. Verbs of Sending and Carrying (Section 11) can be input the following alternations:

(1) Dative Alternation

(2) Conative Alternation

(3) Causative Alternation

(4) Middle Alternation

(5) Coreferential interpretation of pronouns not possible

The Send Verbs of 11.1 and Slide Verbs of 11.2 share the meaning of causing an entity to change location. Bring and Take of 11.3, Carry Verbs of 11.4 and Drive Verbs of 11.5 are all relate to the causation of accompanied motion. The class members of Carry Verbs none of them specify a particular direction of motion. Drive Verbs specify something about the manner of motion especially by the vehicle or means, and some of them even take their name from the vehicle.

For one thing, it is unquestionable that Levin (1993) does a lot of collecting and classifying work according to the verb's syntactic behavior. Her research has laid a good foundation for the study of verb-variant relations. For another thing, there are still some limitations in the research.

Firstly, some typical variants are neglected by Levin. After the collection of data, this thesis is concerned with many typical variants. For example, the variant expressing direction *"send it back"*, which Levin cannot distinguish.

Secondly, the definitions of some alternations are vague and difficult to correspond. For example:

Nora sent the book to Peter.

Levin believes that the actor doesn't move with the object, but this expression can't explain the example sentence reasonably. The final possession of the book is changed but we are not sure whether Nora change her position with the book.

Thirdly, her definition lacks the semantic details to the deliver event. For instance, the meaning components of actor, tool, and object are not included in the definition.

These problems show that the classification and analysis of verbs based only on syntactic behavior is rough and inaccurate. Therefore, it is necessary to introduce the approach of categorizing and semantic analysis of delivery verbs.

Wei (2015) does a research by analyzing the different variants of delivery events, she constructs a conceptual frame to express the conceptual semantics with connectivity between them. Her study explores the shared conceptual content and the specific conceptual content of each variant contained in the conceptual frame, and adjusts Levin (1993)'s Verb Classification according to the corresponding relationship between the verb and the variant to make its corresponding relationship more accurate.

In conclusion, Levin provides a good foundation on data collection and classification according to verbs syntactic behavior and a preliminary interpretation of alternations (variants). But her definition of delivery verbs is not accurate enough, some of alternations 1are neglected in her classification. These limitations indicate an approach that can refine the classification and semantic analysis of delivery verbs are called for.

Wei (2015) does a further study on delivery event by constructing conceptual frame, and makes the corresponding relationship between the verb and the variant more accurate. But the study only involves part of delivery verbs and their variants, and the research on Chinese delivery event is still insufficient.

6.3 The "Conceptual Frame" Analysis to English Delivery Verbs and Their Constructions

In this section, the word "variant" is used in place of "construction", both of which have the same meaning in the book.

6.3.1 Conceptual Content of English Delivery Events

The event referred to in this thesis is the relationship network of conceptual frame of the event, which can be understood as the whole process of action implementation, and expressed as the conceptual frame (event) in Cognitive-Function Approach (Cheng, 2002, 2005, 2006). The conceptual content of English delivery event includes: the action of the actor; the object; the direction of the object; by the means (include body parts or mediator); the movement of the object (an actor could move with the object or not); the change of the object in location, possession and state, which all defined as "final". There are three substances in delivery event that can be observed in real life: the actor, the means and the object. These substances can be seen as conceptual structure that constitutes the conceptual frame of delivery event. The conceptual frame in Cognitive-Function Approach not only includes the action itself expressed by the verb, but also includes the changes of the location and possession of the object caused by the action. Some of these changes are regarded as possible results of actions, so the results of changes cannot be regarded as a whole with actions themselves, but as different semantics of verbs. In the same delivery event, the conceptual meaning generated by these changes is not the inevitable result of the action, but the possible result (Wei, 2015). Please refer to the example:

a. Nora sent the book.

b. Nora sent Peter the book.

c. Nora sent the book from Paris to London.

Example a is the action performed by the actor, emphasizing the action itself. Example b can be marked as "final possession", and example c changes the location of object which can be marked as "final location". Example b and example c are all "final", and they emphasize the results of the move. So delivery events connect to the perceptual and motor system share the conceptual frame:

```
Actor   +   Delivery action   +   Object
Causer  +   Cause   + Object   +  Final
```

6.3.2 Conception Meaning of English Delivery Constructions

The conceptual frame in 6.2.1 specifies the conceptual content of delivery events, which are shared by all delivery variants. Delivery events share conceptual meaning, which not only connect perceptual and motor systems, but also embody different lexical and grammatical structures, and form different variants. In the next parts, the activated conceptual structure of each variant would be named and discussed.

(1) Patient Variant

The patient variant emphasizes the action of delivery, which can be divided into active and passive form, for example:

The postman delivered the letters promptly. [active]

The goods will be delivered at noon tomorrow. [passive]

(*A Dictionary of Current English Usage*, 2003)

The passive patient variant is because of the lack of actor, which usually indicates the actor could be anyone. The action conceptual structure is activated in this conceptual frame, and possible changes are ignored.

```
(Actor)   +   Delivery action   +   Object
...
```

Besides, there is a subgroup called "objective variant", emphasizing the purpose of the delivery action, for example:

Please mail the letter for me.

(*A Dictionary of Current English Usage*, 2003)

According to the frequency of corpus, these variants often used in daily life, especially in description of delivery action and request.

(2) Acquired Variant

The acquired variant is an acquisition process with active and passive form. Its conceptual structure is similar to patient variant, but the conceptual structure of possession is activated.

```
(Actor)   +   Delivery action   +   Object   +   Recipient
```

Causer	+	Cause	+	Object	+	Possession

In this variant, the possession of the object is changed, but it's not sure whether the object reaches the recipient from the cognitive level, for example:

Nora sent the book to Peter. [active]

The book sent to Peter. [passive]

(*English Verb Classes and Alternations,* 1993)

The statistics show Carry Verbs and Drive Verbs are barely used in this variant. Based on that, the corresponding conceptual meaning takes other delivery verbs in common use, which expresses an action, a request and a command.

(3) Original Possession Variant

The original possession variant has the conceptual meaning of the original ownership of the object, and the ownership could be transferred from one to another. The activated components in the action conceptual structure include:

Actor	+	Delivery action	+	Object	+	(Recipient)		
Causer	+	Cause	+	Object	+	Original Possession	+	(Final Direction)

The "final direction" in this part is a kind of trend that the object is moving to the target. For example:

Have you brought a message from her?

(*A Dictionary of Current English Usage*, 2003)

This variant normally represents a process, which emphasizes the possession of the object before changing. Generally, this is a process involves return, inheritance, and the delivery between targets.

(4) Final Possession (double-object) Variant

Unlike the variant that contain conceptual structure of possession mentioned above, this variant clarifies the result of final possession, and its syntactic structure is double-object structure, please compare:

Nora sent the book to Peter.

Nora sent Peter the book.

(*English Verb Classes and Alternations*, 1993)

The syntactic distribution of example sentences is different, so is the corresponding conceptual meaning, and this conceptual frame can be constituted as:

Actor	+	Delivery action	+	Object	+	Recipient
Causer	+	Cause	+	Object	+	Final Possession

This variant because of double-object structure, it is used less frequently in life. We normally use this variant to express a request and the result of delivery.

(5) Original Location Variant

The original location variant shares the similar conceptual frame with the original possession variant, the conceptual structure of possession is correspond to the location, which is:

Actor + Delivery action + Object
Causer + Cause + Object + Original Location + (Final Direction)

Nora sent the book from Paris to London.

(*English Verb Classes and Alternations*, 1993)

In this kind of variation, Levin lists them separately but doesn't classify them. These variants emphasize the location before moving and usually extend to the final direction. According to the data in this thesis, the Drive Verbs use more frequently than other delivery verbs. This variant is used to describe the transfer of objects.

(6) Final Location (double-object) Variant

Based on the analysis above, we can get the following conceptual frame:

Actor + Delivery action + Object
Causer + Cause + Object + Final Location

For example:

He sent home fifteen dollars last week.

(*A Dictionary of Current English Usage*, 2003)

It's a finished result, which the money has arrived at its final location. But it is the same as the other double-object structure, and people used this variant less than other expressions.

(7) Direction Variant

The direction variant emphasizes the direction of the change in location, which in the conceptual structure possession and location is of the same nature, and the only difference lies in the entity of the final. Please compare:

Nora brought the book to Pamcla.

Nora brought the book to the meeting.

(*English Verb Classes and Alternations*, 1993)

Therefore, the conceptual frame of direction variant is:

> Actor + Delivery action + Object + Recipient
>
> Causer + Cause + Object + Direction

All delivery verbs are frequently used in this variant to express a purpose and the process of location changing.

(8) Distance Variant

The distance variant describes the movement distance of the object, which usually is no clear final direction or final location, for example:

The seeds are carried for miles.

(https://fanyi.baidu.com/#en/zh/carried%20for)

> (Actor) + Delivery action + Object
>
> ...

This variant links to the change of location, but emphasizes the distance that the object moved. It not commonly used in Send Verbs but commonly used in other delivery verbs to express the degree of shifting of the object.

(9) Means (mediator) Variant

This variant involves the conceptual meaning of how to deliver the object that neglected by other variants. In here, the mediator usually represents the behavior of delivering made by a specific actor, which we can conclude this conceptual frame:

> Actor + Delivery action + Object
>
> Causer + Cause + Object

Here the actor and the causer coincide with the mediator.

Thank you for the book you sent me <u>through</u> Mrs. Emery.

(*A Dictionary of Current English Usage*, 2003)

The mediator variant emphasizes who does the delivery action that usually done by living things, which not applicable to the Drive Verbs. This variant is commonly used in expressing the actor who completes the delivery action.

(10) Means (instrument) Variant

Compared to the mediator variant, this variant emphasizes the instrument that used in the delivery action. For example:

We will send the goods by rail.

(*A Dictionary of Current English Usage,* 2003)

The activated component is different from above, and the causer here can be seen as instrument.

Actor　+　Delivery action　+　Object　+　Instrument
Causer　+　Cause　+　Object

Because the conceptual meaning of the Slide Verbs such as "bounce" which is hardly in using outer instrument. From a cognitive point of view, Slide Verbs need to be driven by external forces, so they cannot activate the corresponding conceptual structure to form the corresponding conceptual frame.

Its delivery process is not directly controlled by the actor, but indirectly controlled by the instrument. That's the reason why this variant is frequently used to express what a kind of instrument is taken in the delivery action.

(11) Accompanied Variant

The accompanied variant can be divided into two subgroups depending on whether accompanied by person or object, for example:

Nora sent the book with her.

(*English Verb Classes and Alternations*, 1993)

I hand her the nylon gym bag with jeans, socks, underwear and a rugby shirt.

(Corpus of Contemporary American English; https://www.english-corpora.org/coca/)

The objects behind "with" are secondary components in conceptual structure, which activate the conceptual frame as:

Actor　+　Delivery action　+　Object　+　Part
Causer　+　Cause　+　Object

This variant usually indicates the actor or the secondary object moves with the primary object. According to statistics, there are more the variant of person accompanied than that of object accompanied.

(12) Final State Variant

In this variant, the "final state" here, we define it as a relative location before delivering, because the delivery action normally doesn't change the property of the object. There are some examples:

The wounded men were carried away.

(*A Dictionary of Current English Usage*, 2003)

The winch towed the log out of the way.

(*A Dictionary of Current English Usage*, 2003)

The conceptual structure of location is not activated in this conceptual frame, which we can get:

Actor + Delivery action + Object
Causer + Cause + Object + Final state

The conceptual meaning of such variants is usually determined by their prepositional components, such as "out, back and away". This variant is commonly used to express a command and the result of delivery action.

6.4 The "Conceptual Frame" Analysis to Chinese Delivery Verbs and Their Constructions

In this section, the word "variant" is used in place of "construction", both of which have the same meaning in the book.

6.4.1 Conceptual Content of Chinese Delivery Events

In this section, the Chinese delivery verbs are the equivalents of English putting verbs mainly selected from various English-Chinese dictionary.

Based on the study of English delivery events, we can conclude the conceptual content of Chinese delivery event includes: the action of the actor; the object; the means that used in this event; the delivery process; the results of delivery action (include location, possession, and state) which can be defined as "final".

Compared to the conceptual frame of English delivery events, Chinese delivery events share some parts of conceptual structure with that of English. According to Chinese linguistic habits, we usually elide the actor or the object in expression, for example:

把书传上去。

传他手里了。

(*A Dictionary of Chinese Verbs Usage,* 1999)

The same conceptual content in different semantic structures can be expressed by a structure in the conceptual frame (Cheng, 2006). Although there are some omissions in the expression, the subject and object can be defined according to the actual context.

The conceptual frame corresponding Chinese linguistic characteristics is formulated as:

> (Actor) + Delivery action + (Object)
>
> Causer + Cause + Object + Final

6.4.2 Conception Meaning of Chinese Delivery Constructions

Consistent with English delivery events, in this part, we manage to set up a category for the Chinese delivery variants, and analyze their conceptual construction respectively.

(1) Patient Variant

The patient variant expresses the similar meaning which is "A deliver B" or "B is delivered" to English patient variant. It's an action or a process of delivery, which only activating conceptual structure of action, and the conceptual frame is:

> (Actor) + Delivery action + Object
>
> ...

In this variant, the conceptual structure could be displayed by a Chinese phrase instead of a sentence, such as "传球，推车，递纸条". And this is peculiar syntactic structure in Chinese, which we commonly used in the expression of an action, a request and a command.

(2) Target Variant

The target here represents the recipient of the object, which emphasizes who is the recipient of the object in the delivery event. Although according to the semantic content, the possession of an object changes, but this variation is a delivery process, and not sure whether the object reaches the recipient, so it can form such a conceptual framework:

> (Actor) + Delivery action + (Object) + Recipient
>
> Causer + Cause + Object + Possession

For example:

给朋友。

塞给我。

(*A Dictionary of Chinese Verbs Usage,* 1999)

Some of Chinese delivery verbs require an auxiliary word such as "给" to express the conceptual meaning of delivery. By comparing the corpus of English and Chinese, these kind of Chinese delivery verbs usually are corresponding to the English Carry Verbs.

(3) Repetition Variant

As for this kind of variation, it is a rhetorical device in Chinese, some of which means emphasis, some of which means continuity of action, some of which means urgency, some of which means to enhance mood, for example:

再往后传传。

给病人输输血吧。

(*A Dictionary of Chinese Verbs Usage,* 1999)

The activated conceptual structure is similar to the patient variant, therefore, the conceptual frame is:

```
(Actor)  +  Delivery action  +  Object
...
```

The data of corpus shows that the single Chinese delivery word is frequently used to express a request and a command.

(4) Concurrent Variant

The concurrent variant is purposeful and directional, which could possibly change the location or possession of the object. We can constitute the conceptual frame as:

```
(Actor)  +  Delivery action  +  (Object)
Causer  +  Cause  +  Object  +  Location/Possession
```

抬他上山。

(*A Dictionary of Chinese Verbs Usage,* 1999)

把政权移交给你们。

(BLCU Corpus Center; https://bcc.blcu.edu.cn/lang/zh)

This variant is a process of delivery, which commonly used in expressing a request and a command.

(5) Double-object Variant

The double-object structure in Chinese is different from that of English. This variant can be divided into two kinds of variants in its subclass, which we defined as "acquired and final possession". There are examples:

传他一个好球。

还他两本书。

(A Dictionary of Chinese Verbs Usage, 1999)

Because the conceptual meaning is vague in Chinese, we use the syntactic structure to name this variant, and the conceptual frame is as follows:

> (Actor) + Delivery action + Object + Recipient
>
> Causer + Cause + Object + (Final) Possession

Based on the analysis of data, the "final" is decided by the conceptual meaning of the delivery verbs such as "还", and this variant is used less frequently in daily life.

(6) Amount Variant

The amount variant emphasizes the result of the delivery event especially in the number and duration of the delivery action.

传了两回。

搬了十分钟。

(A Dictionary of Chinese Verbs Usage, 1999)

This variant describes the fact that it has been completed, and the causer is not activated in this conceptual frame:

> (Actor) + Delivery action + (Object)
>
> ...

(7) Accomplishment Variant

In this variant, we usually use "了，过" to indicate that the delivery has been completed, for example:

我给他传了一封信。

我帮老王递过信。

(A Dictionary of Chinese Verbs Usage, 1999)

The conceptual structure in here is the same as that of amount variant:

> (Actor) + Delivery action + (Object)
>
> ...

Besides, this variant is widely used in our life.

(8) Location Variant

The location variant involves the change of location, and the word "了" decides whether the object reaches the final location. Please compare:

递他手里。

传他手里了。

(*A Dictionary of Chinese Verbs Usage,* 1999)

Although the object does not exist in the conceptual structure, from the cognitive point of view, the object exists objectively.

> (Actor) + Delivery action + (Object)
>
> Causer + Cause + Object + (Final) Location

This variant expresses the change result of object location in delivery and the target location of the object.

(9) Final State Variant

The final state variant indicates possible results because of the delivery action, or for some reason, the conceptual structure of delivery action cannot be activated by the actor, which change the state of the object. For example:

传没了。

学费交不成了。

(*A Dictionary of Chinese Verbs Usage,* 1999)

> (Actor) + Delivery action + (Object)
>
> Causer + Cause + Object + Final state

This variant is usually negative in delivery action, which expresses to failure or refusal to deliver.

(10) Means Variant

This variant emphasizes the use of means in the delivery process, and it depends on the instrument or path chosen by the actor.

用手传过去。

从陆路运货物。

(*A Dictionary of Chinese Verbs Usage,* 1999)

```
(Actor)  +  Delivery action  +  (Object)  +  Instrument
Causer  +  Cause  +  Object
```

According to the collected corpus, we tend to use our limbs as delivery instruments.

6.5 A Comparative Analysis of English and Chinese Delivery Events and their Constructions

According to the title of each variant that discussed above, we can directly find some similarity and differences between English and Chinese variants. In this section, the word "variant" is used in place of "construction", both of which have the same meaning in the book.

Patient variant can be found in both English and Chinese, they share same conceptual structure and conceptual frame, and the only difference is that the Chinese expression will be more concise.

```
(Actor)  +  Delivery action  +  Object
...
```

English acquired variant and Chinese target variant have a same conceptual frame. In terms of language structure, both of them emphasize the recipient of delivery event, but English acquired variant is more like a delivery process in expression.

```
(Actor)  +  Delivery action  +  (Object)  +  Recipient
Causer  +  Cause  +  Object  +  Possession
```

The differences in expression of double-object construction between English and Chinese variants are due to the differences in language habits. In English, it refers to that the delivery action has been completed, and the object has reached the final location or recipient. In Chinese, it refers to a delivery process which is different from that of English double-object variant. Their conceptual structures share some parts, and the conceptual frame will activate the corresponding part according to the actual situation.

```
(Actor)  +  Delivery action  +  Object  +  Recipient
Causer  +  Cause  +  Object  +  (Final) Possession/ Location
```

The distance variant in English can be included in Chinese amount variant, which all emphasize the degree of delivery event such as how far or how many times the object moves.

> (Actor) + Delivery action + Object
>
> ...

The change of location is contained both in English and Chinese delivery events, and the "final" is determined by syntactic structure (double-object) in English. As for Chinese location variant, it is determined by actual context. Besides, the "original" is not commonly used in Chinese expression.

> Actor + Delivery action + Object
>
> Causer + Cause + Object + (Final) Location

The final state variant and means variant in English and Chinese have same conceptual structure, and some parts could be omitted in expression.

> (Actor) + Delivery action + (Object)
>
> Causer + Cause + Object + Final state
>
> (Actor) + Delivery action + (Object) + Instrument
>
> Causer + Cause + Object

But because of the characteristics of English and Chinese, there are some special variants: repetition variant, accomplishment variant and accompanied variant.

Repetition variant uses repeated Chinese words to enhance mood while English words cannot be used in this way.

> (Actor) + Delivery action + Object
>
> ...

Accomplishment variant has the same conceptual frame above. It represents the delivery action has been accomplished, and we can easily identify this variant by Chinese word "了" and so on.

Accompanied variant usually has the English word "with", which indicates the actor moves with the object while Chinese doesn't have such words.

> Actor + Delivery action + Object + Part
>
> Causer + Cause + Object

In this part, we will make statistics on the frequency of the collected corpus and analyze whether it is commonly used in the expression of daily life.

Patient variant is commonly used in both English and Chinese, and few words like "drive, shuttle" cannot be input to this variant because they are usually to express other action.

In delivery events, most of them involve the change of location and possession. In English, the word "to" which is high frequency in expression, for example:

I send it to you. (Possession)

I send it to there. (Location)

These variants don't give us the detail whether the object reach the "final" while double-object variants do. However, double-variants are hardly suitable for many delivery verbs, especially in Carry Verbs. And the data shows the Drive Verbs have less frequency in possession variants than other delivery verbs.

Means variant in English is usually composed of the word "by" or "through" and Chinese word is "用".

Accomplishment variant is the most frequent because the Chinese word "了" that we use it almost every day.

6.6 Summary to Chapter Six

As a tentative study, this thesis made a comparative analysis of English and Chinese delivery verbs and their variations, based on the study of delivery event and their variants (Levin, 1993). By constructing conceptual frames, the conceptual content of delivery events shared by all delivery variants and the specific conceptual meaning of each delivery variant are explored and theoretically expounded. It examines the feasibility of the Cognitive-Function Approach (Cheng, 2006) of delivery events and makes the corresponding relation between delivery verbs and their variants more accurate. The major findings are as follows:

(1) For the purpose of exploring the delivery events and their variants, this thesis construct the corresponding conceptual frame by collecting a large number of corpus. Through the data analysis both in English and Chinese, the conceptual frames of delivery events and their variants are summarized as follows:

The shared conceptual frame of English delivery event;

| Actor + Delivery action + Object |
| Causer + Cause + Object + Final |

The available conceptual frame of English delivery event;

> Actor + Delivery action + Object + (Instrument)/(Recipient)
>
> Causer + Cause + Object + [(Original possession)/(Original location) + Final possession/ Final direction/ Final location/ Final state]

The shared conceptual frame of Chinese delivery event;

> (Actor) + Delivery action + (Object)
>
> Causer + Cause + Object + Final

The available conceptual frame of Chinese delivery event;

> (Actor) + Delivery action + (Object) + (Instrument)/(Recipient)
>
> Causer + Cause + Object + [Final possession/ Final location/ Final state]

From the above formula, we can find the consistence of the shared conceptual frames and the subtle differences of the available conceptual frames between Chinese and English.

(2) According to the analysis in chapter six, the differences of English and Chinese language and culture lead to the differences of expression and thinking. Therefore, some special variations of both languages are derived. But from a cognitive perspective, most variants share a common conceptual frame. In the expression of daily life, the verbs used in deliver events have their own characteristics.

However, we have to agree that the study has its unavoidable limitations. Because constraints on time and data that the corpus collection is not comprehensive. We have made a further study of English delivery events, while Chinese variants are only a preliminary analysis. But it provides us a good perspective to study other events with a contrastive analysis in English and Chinese.

Chapter Seven The "Conceptual Frame" Analysis to Throwing Event and Its Expressions

——————————————

7.1 Throwing Event and Related Corpus

In the Oxford Advanced Learner's English-Chinese Dictionary (the 7th edition, 2009), the word event is defined as:

1. to make an object, such as a ball, to move quickly through the air by pushing your hand forward quickly and letting the object go.

2. to put something somewhere quickly and carelessly.

3. to push someone or something roughly and violently.

4. (a) to make your opponent fall to the ground in a sport in which you fight. (b) if a horse throws its rider, it makes them fall onto the ground.

5. to suddenly and quickly move your hands, arms, head etc into a new position.

6. to make someone feel very confused.

On the website: https://en.m.wikipedia.org/wiki/Throwing, there is such definition: "Throwing is the launching of a ballistic projectile by hand. This action is only possible for animals with the ability to grasp objects with their hands (mainly primates)." Based on the above definitions, the term throw in our study is "make an object move quickly through the air to get somewhere or the target by pushing your hand or some instrument forward quickly and letting the object go". According to Cheng's viewpoint, the experience of each event would form a schema in the human brain, it means that the relational network of the process of certain event in the conceptual meaning system. In Cognitive-Functional Approach (Cheng, 2002, 2005, 2006), the conceptual content (conceptual meaning) of an event is formulated as the conceptual frame of the event. The conceptual content of throwing event includes: "The action of the actor, through the controlled instrument (outer instrument or body parts of oneself), physically contact the object of the action, which would probably cause some change in the object in location, possession or property". The throwing event can be illustrated by the following chart.

In this section, throwing verbs are mainly selected from the 17th (Verbs of Throwing) and 12th (Verbs of Exerting Force: Push/Pull verbs) classes of verbs in Levin's book: English Verb Classes and

Alternations: A preliminary Investigation (1993:148-156). They are:

Verb classes	
17.1Throw verbs	Bash, Bat, Bunt, Cast, Catapult,Chuck Fire,Flick, Fling,Flip, Hit, Hurl, Kick Knock, Lob, Loft, Nudge, Pass, Pitch Punt, Shoot, Shove, Slam, Slap, Sling Smash, Tap, Throw, Tip, Toss,
17.2 Pelt verbs	Buffet, Bombard, Pelt, Shower, Stone
12 Verbs of Exerting Force:Push/Pull verbs	Draw Heave Jerk Press Pull Push Shove Thrust Tug Yank

These two classes of verbs are all studied under the title of 'throwing verbs' in a broad sense in this thesis because of the interrelatedness of the meaning of these verbs. For example, the 17th class: Verbs of Throwing and the 12 class: Verbs of Exerting Force: Push/Pull verbs in Levin's classification are all concerned as verbs of "instantaneously causing ballistic motion". The strength of the actions expressed by Verbs of Throwing by Impact range from very strong which can cause changes in the objects to not so strong but it still can cause change. Exerting Force Verbs usually express the actions performed with not so much strength but it still can cause change. So these two classes of verbs are actually in a continuum in terms of the action strength they expressed. For example:

a. Billy was kicking a stone around the yard. (https://www.ldoceonline.com/dictionary/kick)

*b. Billy was buffeting a stone around the yard.

*c. Billy was drawing a stone around the yard.

Example a comes from the webpage of Longman Contemporary English. Example b and c cannot be found in any native English book or webpage and based on the judgments of native English speakers such usages are incorrect and unacceptable. Kick and buffet both belong to the 17th class in Levin's classification, and draw belongs to the 12th class.

The research method applied in this section is 'data-driven', and the study would be conducted through corpus collection, classification and analysis.

The corpus collection work is carried out through the following procedures:

(1) To collect sentences patterns (variants) of each throw verb: some of them are taken from *A Dictionary of Current English Usage* (Zhang, 2003) and other dictionaries edited by native English

speakers; some of them are searched and selected from English corpora, such as FrameNet and BNC (British National Corpus); and some of them are found in publications of native English speakers.

(2) To exhaust sentence patterns (variants) of every throw verb: to get a list of all the variants that throw verbs can enter from the sentence patterns collected in procedure (1), and then to repeat procedure (1) to find for each verb all the variants on the list.

After these procedures, all variants for each throw verb are collected and we can observe which variants each verb can enter.

7.2 Levin's Study of Throwing Verbs

The throwing verbs studied in this thesis are mainly selected from Levin's book *English Verb Classes and Alternations: A preliminary Investigation* (1993). Levin analyzed and classified throw verbs under Lexical Semantics.

According to the assumption, syntactic behavior of a verb, especially its expression and interpretation of its arguments is basically determined by its meaning and if this class verbs share the same meaning components they should show the same syntactic behavior, Levin made classification of throwing verbs in terms of their syntactic behavior.

According to Levin's analysis, the 17th class of verbs: Verbs of Throwing and the 12th class of verbs: Verbs of Exerting Force: Push/Pull verbs can enter the following alternations (Levin 1993):

Throwing Verbs:

1. *Steve tossed the ball.*

   (Levin, 1993)

2. Directional Phrase:

   A. *Steve tossed the ball over the fence/into the garden.*

      (Levin, 1993)

   B. *Steve tossed the ball from the tree to the gate.*

      (Levin, 1993)

3. *Steve tossed the ball at Anna.*

   (Levin, 1993)

4. *Steve tossed Anna with the ball. (et. Pelt)*

   (Levin, 1993)

5. Dative Alternation (most verbs):

      A.   Steve tossed the ball to Anna.

      (Levin, 1993)

      B.   Steve tossed Anna the ball.

      (Levin, 1993)

6. With/Against Alternation:

      A.   Steve tossed the ball against the wall.

      (Levin, 1993)

      B.   Steve tossed the wall with ball.

      (Levin, 1993)

7. Conative Alternation:

      A.   Steve tossed the ball.

      (Levin, 1993)

      B.   Steve tossed at the ball.

      (Levin, 1993)

8. Causative Alternations:

      A.   Steve tossed the ball.

      (Levin, 1993)

      B.   The ball tossed.

      (Levin, 1993)

9. Middle Alternations:

      A.   Steve tossed the softball.

      (Levin, 1993)

      B.   Softballs toss easily.

      (Levin, 1993)

10. Zore-related Nominal:

      A.   Toss

      (Levin, 1993)

Push/pull Verbs:

1. *Nora pushed the chair.*

   (Levin, 1993)

2. Conative Alternations:

      A.   Nora pushed the chair.

(Levin, 1993)

    B.   *Nora pushed at/on/against the chair.*

    (Levin, 1993)

3. Causative Alternations:

    A.   *Nora pushed the chair.*

    (Levin, 1993)

    B.   *The chair pushed.*

    (Levin, 1993)

4. Way Object Alternations (some verbs):

    A.   *Nora pushed through the crowd.*

    (Levin, 1993)

    B.   *Nora pushed her way through the crowd.*

    (Levin, 1993)

5. *Nora pushed the chair against the wall.*

    (Levin, 1993)

6. Coreferential interpretation of pronouns possible:

    Nora pushed the chair away from her.

    (Levin, 1993)

7. Resultative Phrase:

    Nora pushed the door shut.

    (Levin, 1993)

The Throw verbs of 17.1, Pelt verbs of 17.2, and Verbs of Exerting Force of 12 share the meaning of "instantaneously causing ballistic motion" of object. It can change the possession, location, final state of an object.

There are many differences between Throw Verbs and Pull/Push Verbs. For example, there is no Directional Phrase Alternation in Push/Pull Verbs. They don't emphasize the direction rather than the Throw Verbs. Also there is no Zore-related Nominal Alternation in Pull/Push Verbs, an object must be in the sentences of Pull/Push Verbs. With/Against Alternation is another difference, the Pull/Push verbs do not show the with/against alternation. These verbs are found in the 'NP V NP with NP' frame, but not found in 'NP V NP against NP' frame. They do not allow instrument subjects.

Levin does a lot in data collection and verbs classification base on their syntactic behavior. Her job sets a good foundation for the studies of verb-variant relations, but there are still some problems in her research.

Firstly, some typical variants which is distinct in the study of verb-variant relations are ignored by Levin. According to the data of this thesis, the variants expressing direction, location and possession change in forms of propositional phrases or ditransitive structures are characteristic of Throw and Push/Pull verbs, which Levin fails to distinguish, for example:

A. *Each archer shot three arrows <u>to the sky.</u>*

(Zhang, 2003)

B. *Shove a boat <u>into the water.</u>*

(Zhang, 2003)

C. *Steve tossed the ball <u>to Anna.</u>*

(Zhang, 2003)

D. *He passed <u>him the bread.</u>*

(Zhang, 2003)

In example *a*, the propositional phrases *to the sky* expresses an obvious direction change caused by the shot action; the propositional phrases *into the water* in example b shows change in location; the propositional phrases *to Anna* in example c shows the possession change; and the ditransitive structure passed *him the bread* shows the possession change.

In addition, based on the data of this thesis, two variants expressing change in property are different, i.e., that in form of adjective phrase and that in form of propositional phrase, For example:

A. *She flung all the windows <u>open.</u>*

(Zhang, 2003)

B. *If the police see the dangerous murder, they'll shoot <u>to kill.</u>*

(Zhang, 2003)

Levin only distinguished the former variant.

Secondly, the definitions of some alternations are fussy. For example, the with alternation, against alternation, and the through alternation obviously have distinct structures and emphasize different components in these kinds of variants, but Levin still defined them as with/against alternation and through/with alternation. These should be classified into different alternations while Levin does not do this job. It does not clear the way for the readers to understand these verbs. Moreover, Levin does not pay attention to the minute differences in the meaning of variants caused by different participants. For example:

A. *He cast a <u>stone</u> against the window.*

(Zhang, 2003)

B. He cast a <u>stick</u> against the window.

The two sentences have the same syntactic structure but they emphasize different participants of the action. The former emphasizes the change in the instrument '*stone*', while the latter emphasizes the change in the object 'stick'.

These problems show that to classify and analyze these verbs base on the syntactic behavior is rough and inaccurate. Therefore, to introduce the new approaches which can refine the classification and the semantic analysis of Throw verbs is necessary.

Levin does a lot in data collection and verbs classification base on their syntactic behavior. Her job gives a good base for studies in verb-variant relations, but there are problems in her study of throw verbs. Firstly, some typical variants which is distinct in the study of verb-variant relations are ignored by Levin. Secondly, the definitions of some alternations are fussy. Thirdly, Levin does not pay attention to the minute differences in the meaning of variants caused by different participants.

These problems found in this study under Lexical semantics indicate that it is necessary to find more precise and effective models to refine the classification and semantic analysis.

7.3 The "Conceptual Frame" Analysis to English Throwing Verbs and Their Constructions

In this section, the word "variant" is used in place of "construction", both of which have the same meaning in the book.

7.3.1 Conceptual Content of English Delivery Events

Event here means the relational network of the very event in the conceptual system, which is formulated as conceptual frame in Cognitive-Functional Approach (Cheng, 2006). The conceptual content of throw event includes: "The action of the actor, through the controlled instrument (outer instrument or body parts of oneself) to move the object to another object (target) or somewhere and it would probably cause some changes in the object in location, possession or property". Location, possession and property are all generalized as "final".

In real world, three or four substances can be seen in throw event: the actor, the instrument, and the object, the target or somewhere, and at the same time the action, the movement and the possible changes can be observed. The action of throw or push/pull is regarded as the influence(movement) which the actor exert to the object to let it get somewhere or the target. The conceptual meanings of confrontation and change are equivalent to Talmy's Force-dynamics schema concerning the interaction between antitrope and antagonist. And in terms of the conceptual domain, the changes of object in location, possession and property can be specialized. Please compare:

He kick the ball <u>into the room.</u>   [final location]

(Corpus of Contemporary American English; https://www.english-corpora.org/coca/)

He kicked <u>her</u> a ball.   [final possession]

(http://www.lintroduction.com/Article_Show.asp?ArticleID=181)

He kicked her <u>black and blue.</u>   [final property]

(http://query.nytimes.com/gst/abstract.html?res=F40A11F63B59107B93C1A91783D85F448784F9)

These three kinds of changes are marked location, possession and property respectively. They are all 'final'. The shared conceptual content of the Throw event, which connects with the perceptual and locomotor system, can be represented in this conceptual frame:

Actor	+ Throw Action+Instrument +Object+Destination/target	
Causer	+ Cause	+Patient +Final

Here the actor coincides with the causer, and the object coincides with the patient.

7.3.2 Conception Meaning of English Delivery Constructions

The conceptual frame in 7.3.1 formulates the conceptual content of Throw event, which is shared by all the Throw variants. On one hand such conceptual content connects with the perceptual and locomotor system, and on the other hand it can be construed as various variants. The conceptual meanings of throwing variants are formulated as the elaboration of the generalized throwing conceptual frame.

There are various variants representing the throwing event. According to the viewpoints of Cheng, as a relational network, the activation of different paths in the conceptual frame would be embodied as different grammatical structures, and the activation of the path is represented as the activation of certain semantic components, such as the participants. In the following part, the activated components of each variant would be discussed respectively.

(1) The Class of Action Variants

This class of variants emphasize the state in which "the throw action involves the object", while the conceptual content of change in object is neglected. In conceptual frame, only the action conceptual structure is activated, and the causative conceptual structure is inactivated (In the following frame the bold parts mark the possibly activated components).

> **Actor + Throw action +Instrument + [Object + Part+Target/Destination]**
>
> (Causer+Cause   + [Patient   + [Goal/Final direction and location /Resistance] /[Final direction/Final possession]/[Final property₁/final property₂]])
>
> /(Causer+Cause   + [Object+ [Final direction or location/Resistance]])

The class of transitive action variants can be divided into three subgroups, and they are transitive action alteration, instrument alteration and part variant, all of which exclude the conceptual meaning of change in object. For example:

Please pass the salt.   [transitive action variant]

(Zhang, 2003)

He tapped the table <u>with his pencil.</u>   [instrument variant]

(Zhang, 2003)

Jean raised her hand and slapped the boy <u>on the face.</u> [part variant]

(Zhang, 2003)

1) Transitive Action Variant

Generally, the instrument participant would not be activated in transitive action alteration, but when the verbs (such as whip and belt) which simultaneously express action and instrument enter this variant the instrument would be activated. In this thesis, we call those verbs as whip and belt compound verb. We can compare:

A. The men were pitching hay.

(Zhang, 2003)

B. This police shoots the target.

The instrument in clause A would not be activated and represented, while in clause B both the instrument gun and the action of gun are activated. The activated components in the action conceptual structure include:

Transitive Action Alteration: *This police shoots the target.*

> **Actor** he + **Throw action** + (**Instrument** shoot) + [**Object** target + Part]
>
> ……

Here the action and the instrument are represented compoundedly by the verb *shoot*.

2) Instrument Variant

The instrument variant doesn't activate causative conceptual structure. Body-part of the object is also not activated. The instrument is the obligatorily activated part which is represented as *with* prepositional phrase, for Example:

[Instrument Alteration ₁]: *You've hit that bird with your last shot.*

(Corpus of Contemporary American English)

> **Actor** he + **Throw action** hit + (**Instrument shot**) + [**Object** bird + Part]

Though the activated components in instrumental variant are the same as these in transitive action alteration expressed by compound verb (such as shoot which simultaneously express action and instrument), the action and instrument in instrumental variant are represented as verb and with prepositional phrase respectively. Of course, the instrument variant also promises the blended representational relation of action and instrument, for example:

[Instrument Alteration₂]: *He shoots the bird with his last shoot.*

(Corpus of Contemporary American English)

> **Actor** he + **Throw action** + (**Instrument** his last shoot) + [**Object** bird + Part]
>
> ......

Here the instrument participant is represented as with prepositional phrase, and at the same time instrument blends with the throw action as the verb shoot. According to the economical principle, when a participant has two different representations simultaneously there must be certain kinds of semantic metonymy between them, or the clause would be regarded as improper by the native speakers. We can compare:

A. *He shoots the bird with his last shoot.*

(Corpus of Contemporary American English)

B. *He shoots the bird with at shoot.*

(Corpus of Contemporary American English)

3) Part Variant

In part variant, instrument is an optional component, while the object must be activated and represented as the prepositional phrase in the end of the clause.

He hit the ball on the red spot.   [Part variant]

> **Actor** he + **Throw action** hit + (Instrument) + [**Object** 1 + **Part** red spot]

93

(2) The Class of Change in Object Variants

The variants in this class share a common characteristic that the object is salient in the variants and the change in the object is overtly represented. So in conceptual frame, the causative conceptual structure representing change in object must be activated.

The throw action may cause various changes in the object, which in terms of conceptual domain can be classified into three types: change in location, possession, and property. In the mental operation of throw event, only one kind of change would be activated, for example:

He kick the ball into the room.   [final location]

He kicked her a ball.   [final possession]

(http://www.lintroduction.com/Article_Show.asp?ArticleID=181)

He kicked her black and blue.   [final property]

(http://query.nytimes.com/gst/abstract.html?res=F40A11F63B59107B93C1A91783D85F448784F9)

Here, choice would be made from these three conceptual domains (in the conceptual frame it is marked by "/"). The mental operation of change in object variants only activates action conceptual structure and the first causative structure in conceptual frame. The 'object part' in the action structure is not activated. (In the following frame the bold parts mark the possibly activated components)

Actor + **Throw action** +Instrument + [**Object** + Part]

(Causer+Cause   + [**Patient**   + [**Goal/Final direction and location /Resistance**]

/[**Final direction/Final possession**]/[**Final property1/final property2**]])

/(Causer+Cause   + [Object+ [Final direction or location/Resistance]])

According to conceptual domain, variants are classified into three kinds, and within each domain there are different variants.

1) Location Domain

The variants representing change in location include goal variant, final location (and direction) variant, and resist variant, for example:

Each archer shoot three arrows at the target.   [goal variant]

(Zhang, 2003)

He kick the ball into the room.   [final direction and location variant]

(Zhang, 2003)

He shot the arrow from the bow.   [Original Location]

(Zhang, 2003)

My documents were passed from one official to another.   [Original   Location-Final   Location

variant]

(Zhang, 2003)

He cast a stone against the window.   [resist variant]

(Zhang, 2003)

The goal variant represents the assumed goal of the moving path of the object, i.e., the mental aiming of the goal; the final direction and location variant represents the moving process (final direction) and ending position (final location) of the object; the original location variant or original location-Final location variant represents the moving process(direction: original location-final location) and ending position of the object; and the resist variant represents the confrontation of the power between the object and the final location entity. The goal variant, final location (and direction) variant, and resist variant are differentiated within the location domain, but only one of them is activated in the mental operation of a throw event, for example:

Final Direction and Location Variant: *He kick the ball into the room.*

Actor + **Throw action** +**Instrument** + [**Object** + Part]

(**Causer+Cause**   + [**Patient**   + [Goal/**Final direction and location**/original location-

final location /Resistance]/[Final direction/Final possession]/[Final property$_1$/final property$_2$]])

/(**Causer+Cause**   + [Object+ [Final direction or location/Resistance]])

---

2) Possession Domain

Within possession domain, mainly there are two kinds of variants. They are final direction variant and final possession variant, and only one of them would be activated in the mental operation.

He kicked the ball <u>to her</u>.   [final direction variant]

(http://www.english-for-students.com/Prepositions-1.html)

He kicked <u>her</u> a ball.   [final possession variant]

(Zhang, 2003)

The conceptual meanings of these two kinds of variants are different. Final direction variant emphasizes the direction of the change in possession, while final possession variant emphasizes the ending of the change and the acquisition of the object by the final possessor. For example:

[Final Possession Variant]: *He kicked <u>her</u> a ball.*

> **Actor** + **Throw action** +**Instrument** + [**Object** + Part]
>
> (**Causer+Cause**   + [**Patient**   + [Goal/Final direction and location /Resistance]/[Final direction/**Final possession**]/[Final property1/final property2]])
>
> /(Causer+Cause   + [Object+ [Final direction or location/Resistance]])

Besides, final direction variants in possession domain and location domain are of the same nature, and the only difference lies in the entity of the final. Please compare:

A. He kicked the ball to her.   [final direction variant- possession]

(http://www.english-for-students.com/Prepositions-1.html)

B. He kick the ball into the room.   [final location]

The final of clause A is *her* which belongs to possession domain, while the final of clause B is room which belongs to location domain.

3) Property Domain

Property change in object caused by throw action can be represented by two kinds of variants:

She flung all the windows open.   [Final property variant1]

If the police see the dangerous murder, they'll shoot to death.   [Final property variant2]

(Zhang, 2003)

Final property variant1 use adjective or adverb to represent the final property, and final property variant2 use propositional phrase to represent the final property. In mental operation only one kind of variant would be activated, for example:

[Final Property Variant1- Adjective]: *She beat him black and blue.*

> **Actor** + **Throw action** +**Instrument** + [**Object** + Part]
>
> (**Causer+Cause**   + [**Patient**   + [Goal/Final direction and location /Resistance]/[Final direction/Final possession]/[**Final property**1/final property2]]) / (Causer+Cause   + [Object+ [Final direction or location/Resistance]])

In conclusion, change the object variants all emphasize the object and the change in object caused by Throw action. The highlighted objects are all represented as the noun phrases in the object position of the clause. The instruments are neglected, sometimes having no overt expression in the clause.

(3) The Class of Change in Instrument Variants

In this class the instrument is salient in the variants and the change in instrument is overtly represented. In the form-meaning representational relation, the emphasis of the instrument is the overt representation of the moving process and final location of the instrument, or the representation of the power opposition between the instrument and the final location entity. These two kinds of representations formed two variants in this class: final direction and location variant and resistance variant:

A. The men were pitching hay.

(Zhang, 2003)

B. This police shoots the target.

(Corpus of Contemporary American English; https://www.english-corpora.org/coca/)

In conceptual frame, change in instrument is mainly represented by the second causative conceptual structure. The object in this causative conceptual frame coincides with the instrument in the action structure, and its final (the final direction and location/resistance in the frame) coincides with the action object. In the mental operation process, both the action conceptual structure and the second causative structure are activated, with the first causative structure half activated, for example:

[Instrument resistance variant]: *He cast a stone against the window.*

> **Actor + Throw action +Instrument + [Object + Part]**
>
> (Causer+Cause   + [Patient   + [Goal/Final direction and location /Resistance] /[Final direction/Final possession]/[Final property1/final property2]])
>
> / (**Causer+Cause**   + [**Object**+ [Final direction or location/**Resistance**]]

Except the subject, one clause only emphasizes one participant which is represented as the noun phrase in the object position of the clause. The emphasized participant corresponds to the 'trajector' in Langacker's theory (1987, 1990, 1991). The components of object complement further illustrate the conceptual content of the participant which equals to Langacker's 'landmark'. It is observed that no matter it emphasizes the object or the instrument, there exist final direction and location and resistance in the landmark. Of course, there is difference between the landmark of the change in object variants and the change in instrument variants, i.e., the landmark object can be goal, but goal cannot be the landmark of instrument. Cheng suggests that this difference in the landmark of object and instrument basically corresponds to the human experiences in the world. The instrument, which is controlled by the actor, can easily hit the object, so goal variant which emphasizes the "assumed goal of the object" does not belong to the class of change in instrument variants; while the arrival of the object at the goal position is much more difficult for its moving process is not directly controllable by the actor. The different experiences of people in the world are represented as different variants in English language.

(4) Driven Variant and Beneficiary Variant

In this two class, the motivation and the beneficiary of the action will be emphasized while the object will be neglected in some occasions. The emphasis of the motivation and beneficiary make them different from other variants. For example:

The people shoved <u>to get on the crowded car.</u> [Driven Variant]

(Zhang, 2003)

He's ready to go to <u>bat for you.</u> [Beneficiary Variant]

(Zhang, 2003)

Actor + **Throw action** +**Instrument** + [Object + Part]+[**motivation/beneficiary**]

(Causer+Cause + [Patient + [**motivation/beneficiary**])

Through the construction of conceptual frames, the general conceptual content of throw event which is shared by all the throw variants and the specific conceptual meaning of each throw variant are theoretically formulated. Thus the correspondence between throw verbs and their variants are clearly illustrated. A revision to Levin (1993)'s classification of the throw verbs is made based on the study of throw verbs under the Cognitive-Functional Approach (Cheng, 2006).

7.4 The "Conceptual Frame" Analysis to Chinese Throwing Event and Its Constructions

In this section, the word "variant" is used in place of "construction", both of which have the same meaning in the book.

7.4.1 "Final" Class Constructions of Chinese Throw Event

The conceptual content of Chinese throw event also includes: "The action of the actor, controlled instrument (outer instrument or body parts of oneself) to move the object to another object(target) or somewhere and it would probably cause some changes in the object in location, possession or property". Location, possession and property are all generalized as "final".

In section 7.3, we can know, in real world, three or four substances can be seen in English throw event. It is the same in Chinese throw event: the actor, the instrument, and the object, the target or somewhere, and at the same time the action, the movement and the possible changes can be observed. The 'final' in English throw event means" location, procession, and property". There are some differences in Chinese. Not only the "final" but also the direction and moving trend can be regarded as "final". Please compare:

他把球从半场踢进了球门。[original location-final location]

(from the native speakers)

他把球丢地上了。[final location]

(*A Dictionary of Chinese Verb Usage*, 1999)

一头把他撞了出去。[moving trend]

(*A Dictionary of Chinese Verb Usage*, 1999)

他把球踢到左边了。[final direction]

(*A Dictionary of Chinese Verb Usage*, 1999)

他把球投向队友。[final possession]

(*A Dictionary of Chinese Verb Usage*, 1999)

这个人被汽车撞成残废了。[final property]

(*A Dictionary of Chinese Verb Usage*, 1999)

Direction and moving trend can be also added to "final". They all are "final". They shared conceptual content of the Chinese throwing event, these variants can be represented in this conceptual frame:

Actor + Instrument + **Throw Action** + **Object** + **Destination/target**
Causer + Cause +Patient +[original location-final location/final location/moving trend/final direction/final possession/final property] +Destination/Target

7.4.2 Times Construction and Duration Construction

In Chinese throw events, the throw actions would not act only one times in some occasions. In this class, times or time which the action acts will be emphasized. For example:

这球踢了两个小时了。[duration variant]

(*A Dictionary of Chinese Verb Usage*, 1999)

我撞了门三下儿。[duration variant]

(*A Dictionary of Chinese Verb Usage*, 1999)

The emphasis of the times and length of time of the throw action makes them different from other class, these variants can be represented in this conceptual frame:

Actor + Instrument + **Throw Action** + **Object** +[Destination/target] + **duration/times**
Causer + Cause +Patient [Destination/target] + **duration/times**

7.5 A Comparative Analysis of English and Chinese Throwing Events and their Constructions

According to the analysis in 7.3 and 7.4, it could be find that throwing verbs in Chinese and English they have the same variants: final location variant, final procession variant, final property variant. In some throw events, the action of the actor, through the controlled instrument (outer instrument or body parts of oneself) to move the object to another object(target) or somewhere and it would probably cause some changes in the object in location, possession or property". Location, possession and property are all generalized as "final". While in Chinese, 'final' means more, *moving trend variant and final direction variant* are also the members of 'final'. English frame:

Actor + Throw action +Instrument + [Object + Part]+Destination/Target
(Causer+Cause + [Patient + [Goal/Final direction and location /Resistance]/[Final direction/Final possession]/[Final property1/final property2]])
/(Causer+Cause + [Object+[Original location-final location/Final direction or location/Resistance]]) +Destination/Target

Chinese frame:

Actor + Instrument + Throw Action + Object + Destination/target
Causer + Cause +Patient +[original location-final location/final location/moving trend/final direction/final possession/final property] +Destination/Target

On the other hand, both English throwing verbs and Chinese throwing verbs have some special variants which cannot be concluded into the same frame with other variants. Moreover, these variants are not the same in English and Chinese. These variants in English: *Driven Variant and Beneficiary Variant.* They shared the same frame:

Actor + **Throw action** +**Instrument** + [Object + Part]+**[motivation/beneficiary]**
(Causer+Cause   + [Patient   + **[motivation/beneficiary**])

These variants in Chinese: *Times Variant and duration variant.* They shared the same frame:

Actor + Instrument + **Throw Action** + **Object** +[Destination/target] + **duration/times**
Causer   + Cause   +Patient   [Destination/target] + **duration/times**

There are some differences between English 'final' class variants and Chinese 'final' class variants. The 'final' class variants of English mainly focus on the *location, possession and property* domains, while Chinese 'final' class variants have more types: moving trend and final direction. The frame of Chinese 'final' class variants are presented as:

Actor + Instrument + **Throw Action** + **Object** + **Destination/target**
Causer   + Cause   +Patient +[original location-final location/final location/moving trend/final direction/final possession/final property] +Destination/Target

The frame of English 'final' class variants:

Actor + Throw action +Instrument + [**Object** + Part]
(Causer+Cause   + **[Patient**   + **[Goal/Final direction and location /Resistance]** /**[Final direction/Final possession]**/**[Final property1/final property2]**]) /(Causer+Cause + [Object+ [Final direction or location/Resistance]])

7.6 Summary to Chapter Seven

The objective of this section is to discuss the semantic correspondence between the throwing verbs and their variants under the "Conceptual Frame" Approach (Cheng, 2002, 2005, 2006).

In this section, conceptual frames were constructed to explore and theoretically formulate the conceptual content of the throw event which is shared by all the throw variants and the specific conceptual meaning of each kind of throw variant through which the semantic correspondence between throw verbs and their variants would be illustrated by the study of such form-meaning semiotic relation. And based on this, the contrast between Cognitive-Functional Approach and Construction Grammar can be drawn.

The conceptual content of throw event includes: "The action of the actor, through the controlled instrument (outer instrument or body parts of oneself), throw the object of the action to the destination or target, it would probably cause some change in the object in location, possession or property." The shared conceptual content of the throw event, which connects with the perceptual and locomotor system, can be represented in the following conceptual frame:

| Actor + throw action +Instrument +Object + Destination/Target |
| Causer + Cause +Patient + Indirect object/Location +Final |

There are various variants representing the throw event, and such variety is firstly manifested in different topics. The actor-topiced variants are the main focus of this thesis. These variants are grouped into four classes. The first three conceptual frame concerning these variants is formulated as:

Actor + Throw action +Instrument + [Object + Part]+Destination/Target

(Causer+Cause + [Patient + [Goal/Final direction and location /Resistance]/[Final direction/Final possession]/[Final property1/final property2]])

/(Causer+Cause + [Object+[Original location-final location/Final direction or location/Resistance]]) +Destination/Target

The frame of Driven Variant and Beneficiary Variant:

Actor + Throw action +Instrument + [Object + Part]+[**motivation/beneficiary**]

(Causer+Cause + [Patient + [**motivation/beneficiary**])

The class of transitive action variants emphasize the "involvement of the object by the throw action", while the conceptual content of the change in the object is weakened. In its conceptual frame only the action conceptual structure is activated with the causative conceptual structure remaining inactivated (In the following conceptual frame the bold parts mark the possibly activated components).

Actor + Throw action +Instrument + [**Object + Part**]+ **Destination/Target**

(Causer+Cause + [Patient + [Goal/Final direction and location /Resistance] /[Final direction/Final possession]/[Final property1/final property2]])

/(Causer+Cause + [Object+ [Final direction or location/Resistance]]) +Indirect object/Location

This class of variants are divided into three subgroups, all of which exclude the conceptual meaning of change in object.

[The transitive action alteration]: *This police shoots the bird.*

> **Actor** police + **Throw action** + (**Instrument** gun) + [**Object** bullet+ Part]+ (**Destination/Target** bird)
>
> ......

[Instrument alteration₁]: *He shoot the bird with his gun.*

> **Actor** he + **Throw action** shoot + (**Instrument** his gun) + [**Object** bullet + Part]+ (**Destination/Target** bird)
>
> ......

[Instrument alteration₂]: *He shoot the bird with his last shoot.*

> **Actor** he + **Throw action** + (**Instrument** *his last shoot*) + [**Object** bullet + Part]+(**Destination/Target** bird)
>
> ......

[Part variant]: *He hit the all on the red spot.*

> **Actor** he + **Throw action** hit + (Instrument) + [**Object** ball + **Part** red spot]
>
> ......

The cognitive operation of the changes in the object variants only activates action conceptual structure and the first causative structure in the frame. But the "object part" in the action structure is not activated. (In the following frame the bold parts mark the possibly activated components)

> **Actor + Throw action +Instrument + [Object + Part]**
> **(Causer+Cause + [Patient + [Goal/Final direction and location /Resistance]**
> **/[Final direction/Final possession]/[Final property₁/final property₂]]) + Destination/Target**
> /(Causer+Cause + [Object+ [Final direction or location/Resistance]]) +Indirect object/Location

Three kinds of variants can be distinguished in this class of variants according to conceptual domain: location domain, possession domain, and property domain (as is shown in the above conceptual frame).

In the conceptual frame, change in the instrument is mainly represented by the second causative conceptual structure. The object in this causative conceptual frame coincides with the instrument in the action structure, and its final (the [Final direction and location/Resistance] in the frame) coincides with the action object. In the cognitive operation process, both the action conceptual structure and the second causative structure are activated, with the first causative structure being half activated, for example:

[instrument resistance variant]: *He cast a stone against the window.*

> **Actor + Throw action +Instrument + [Object + Part]+ Destination/Target**
>
> (Causer+Cause   + [Patient   + [Goal/Final direction and location /Resistance]
> /[Final direction/Final possession]/[Final property1/final property2]])
>
> / (**Causer+Cause**   + [**Object**+ [Final direction or location/**Resistance**]])   +Indirect
> object/Location

Then, the writer summarizes the Chinese throwing verb variants and constructs their frames. First, *original location-final location variant, final location, moving trend variant, final direction variant, final possession variant and final property variant* can be classified into one type:' *Final'*. They share the same frame:

> **Actor   +   Instrument +   Throw Action +   Object   + Destination/target**
> Causer   + Cause   +Patient   +[original location-final location/final location/moving
> trend/final direction/final possession/final property]   +Destination/Target

Next, Times and duration variants share the frame:

> **Actor   +   Instrument +   Throw   Action   +   Object   +[Destination/target] +**
> **duration/times**
>   Causer   +   Cause   +Patient   [Destination/target]   +
> **duration/times**

Then, the writer compares the throwing verbs variants and frames in Chinese and English to find their similarities and their differences. It is found that throw verbs in Chinese and English they all have the same variants: final location variant, final procession variant, final property variant. In some throw events, the action of the actor, through the controlled instrument (outer instrument or body parts of oneself) to move the object to another object(target) or somewhere and it would probably cause some changes in the object in location, possession or property". Location, possession and property are all generalized as "final". While in Chinese, 'final' means more, *moving trend variant and final direction variant* are also the members of 'final'. Both English throwing verbs and Chinese throwing verbs have some special variants which cannot be concluded into the same frame with other variants. Moreover, these variants are not the same in English and Chinese. These variants in English: *Driven Variant and Beneficiary Variant.*

These variants in Chinese: *Times Variant and duration variant.*

Through the construction of conceptual frames, the general conceptual content of the Throw event which is shared by all the Throw variants and the specific conceptual meaning of each kind of Throw variant are described and theoretically formulated. Thus the correspondence between Throw verbs and their variants are clearly illustrated.

Chapter Eight Conclusion

Under the perspective of the Embodied Language of Cognition (Glenberg, 1997; Barsalou, 1999; Anderson, 2003), this book proposes a theoretical framework (hypothesis): the form-meaning relation in language shall be a three-dimensional interactive relation between body (the sensory-motor system) — brain (the mental network of the experiential knowledge) — form (the language expression system), rather than be a two dimensional relation between meaning and form. Body is the original source of "meaning". The specific "meaning" comes from the body (the sensory-motor practices), (which becomes a part of the experiential knowledge network) stored in the brain and embodied as certain language form (expression); at the same time, the processing of certain language expression needs to extract the "meaning" (related experiential knowledge) from the brain, which in turn actives the "meaning" (related sensory-motor experiences) from the body. The brain is the core of the three-dimensional interactive relation, which joints the body and the language expression.

Taking the obtaining event and its constructions as examples, the present book used the "Body—Brain—Form" Approach to explain the construal mechanism of the obtaining construction, that is, interpreted the three-dimensional construal processes from the source of the specific "meaning", i.e., the sensory-motor practices of obtaining, to specific obtaining constructions, with brain experiential knowledge network being the joint between the former two aspects. The core conceptual content of the obtaining event is: the actor (i.e., the obtainer) obtains or gets something (i.e., the obtained object) (from other people, i.e., the original owner of the obtained object). This is the part of the experiential knowledge network related with all the sensory-motor practices of obtaining and the processing of any obtaining construction would activate. Considering specific sensory-motor practices of obtaining actions, the elaborated conceptual content of the obtaining event could be conclude as: for some purposes, the actor (i.e., the obtainer) obtains or gets something (i.e., the obtained object) from other people or location (i.e., the original owner or location of the obtained object), by certain approach, using certain instrument (one's body or outer instrument), or paying certain price; this would cause the change of the possession of the obtained object and may cause the change of location or property of the object; sometimes, the obtaining purpose may be realized by exchange. The elaborated conceptual content of the obtaining event contains the core conceptual content of this event. Different sensory-motor practices of obtaining are stored in the brain to form different parts (paths) of the obtaining knowledge network and are construed as different obtaining verbs and constructions. The Processing of different obtaining constructions would activate different paths of the obtaining knowledge network in the brain, which in turn activate specific obtaining sensory-motor experiences. This explanation system could predicate the usage distribution of different obtaining constructions, the rationality and accuracy of which were proved by the quantitative analysis. This book also adopted the Cognitive Event Frame (Cheng, 2019, 2020) to formulate the core conceptual content and the elaborated conceptual content of the obtaining event, proving that this approach could formulize the content of the experiential knowledge stored in the brain, which is economical in description and flexible in application.

Besides, this book also reports several data analysis cases under the framework of the Conceptual Frame approach (Cheng, 2002, 2005, 2006) to further verify the effectiveness of this approach in formulating conceptual contents, including the analysis on the physical contact event and its (English) constructions and the comparative analysis on the throwing event and its Chinese and English constructions and that on the delivery event and its Chinese and English constructions.

Bibliography

————————————

Anderson, M. L. Embodied cognition: a field guide[J]. *Artificial Intelligence*, 2003, 149 (1): 91-130.

Barsalou L. W. Perceptual symbol systems[J]. *Behavioral and Brain Sciences*, 1999, 22 (4): 577-660.

Chomsky, Noam. *Lectures on Government and Binding* [M]. Dordrecht: Foris, 1981.

Chomsky, Noam. *Knowledge of Language* [M]. New York: Praeger, 1986.

Chomsky, Noam. *New Horizons in the Study of Language and Mind* [M]. Cambridge: Cambridge University Press, 2000.

Fillmore, C.J. The case for case [C]. In *Universals in Linguistic Theory*. eds. Emmon Bach and Robert Harms. New York: Holt, Rinehart, and Winston, 1968.

Fillmore C. J. Frame Semantics [C]. In *Linguistics in the Morning Calm*, eds. The Linguistics Society of Korea. Seoul: Hanshin, 1982: 111-137.

Fillmore C. J. Lowe J. B, Baker C.F. *A Frame-Semantic Approach to Semantic Annotation* [M]. Berkeley: University of California, International Compute Science Institute and Department of Linguistics, 1997.

Goldberg, Adele. *Constructions: A Construction Grammar Approach to Argument Structure* [M]. Chicago: The University of Chicago Press, 1995.

Goldberg, A. & Suttle, L. Construction grammar [J]. *Wiley Interdisciplinary Reviews Cognitive Science*, 2010(4), 468-477.

Glenberg, A. M. What memory is for[J]. *Behavioral and Brain Sciences*, 1997, 20 (1): 1-19.

Halliday, M. A. K. *An Introduction to Functional Grammar* [M]. 2nd edn. London: Edward Arnold, 1994

Hale, K. L. & Keyser, S. J. Prolegomenon to a Theory of Argument Structure [J]. *American Journal of Epidemiology*, 1999 (2):127-128.

Jackendoff, R.S. *Semantic Structures* [M]. Cambridge, Massachusetts: The MIT Press, 1990.

Jackendoff, R. S. *Foundations of Language: Brain, Meaning, Grammar Evolution* [M]. New York: Oxford University Press, 2002

Jackendoff, R. S. *Language, Consciousness, Culture: Essays on Mental Structure* [M]. Cambridge, Mass.: MIT Press, 2007

Lamb, S. *Outline of Stratificational Grammar*[M]. Georgetown University Press, 1966.

Lamb, S. *Pathways of the Brain: The Neurocognitive basis of Language* [M]. Amsterdam: John Benjamins Publishing Co, 1999.

Lakoff, G. *Women, Fire, and Dangerous Things* [M]. Chicago: The University of Chicago Press, 1987.

Lakoff, G. Mapping the Brain's Metaphor Circuitry: Metaphorical Thought in Everyday Reason [M]. *Frontiers in Human Neuroscience,* 2014(8): 958.

Langacker, R.W. *Foundations of Cognitive Grammar* [M]. Stanford: Stanford University Press, 1987.

Langacker, R. W. *Concept, Image, and Symbol* [M], Mouton de Gruyter, Berlin, 1990.

Langacker, R. W. *Foundation of Cognitive Grammar 2: Descriptive Application* [M]. Stanford: Stanford University Press, 1991.

Levin, B. *English Verb Classes and Alternations: A Primary Investigation* [M]. Chicago and London: The University of Chicago Press, 1993.

Levin, B. and M. Rappaport Hovav. Wipe the Slate Clean: A Lexical Semantic Exploration [J]. *Cognition.* Vol 41, 1991:123-151.

Levin, B. and M. Rappaport Hovav. *Unaccusativity: At the Syntax-Lexical Semantic Interface* [M]. Cambridge: MIT Press, 1995.

Levin, B. and M. Rappaport Hovav. Building verb meanings [C]. In *The projection of arguments: Lexical and compositional factors*, eds. Miriam Butt and Wilhelm Geuder, 97-134. Stanford, CA: CSLI Publications, 1998.

Levin, B. and M. Rappaport Hovav. *Two Structures for Compositionally Derived Events*[C], In Proceedings of SALT. Stanford, 1999:14.

Levin, B. and M. Rappaport Hovav. *Argument Realization* [M]. Cambridge, MA: The M1T Press, 2005.

Maria Aloni, Paul Dekker, & Floris Roelofsen (eds.), *Proceedings of the 16th Amsterdam Colloquium.* University of Amsterdam, Amsterdam, 2016.

Martin, A., Wiggs, C. L., Ungerleider, L. G., et al. Neural correlates of category-specific knowledge[J]. *Nature*, 1996, 379 (6566): 649-652.

Pinker, S. *Learnability and Cognition: The Acquisition of Argument Structure* [M]. Cambridge, MA: The M1T Press, 1989.

Rappaport Hovav, M. and B. Levin. *Building Verb Meanings* [C], eds. M. Butt and W. Geuder, 1998: 97-134.

Rappaport Hovav, M. and B. Levin. An Event Structure Account of English Resultatives [J]. *Language*, Vol 77, 2001.

Ritter, Elizabeth, and Sara Thomas Rosen. The Projection of Arguments: Lexical and Compositional

Factors. In *Delimiting Events in Syntax*. eds. Butt and Geuder. Stanford California: CSLI Publication, 1998:135-164.

Talmy, L. Path to Realization: A Typology of Event Conflation [C], In *Proceedings of the Seventeenth Annual Meeting of the Berkeley Linguistics Society*. Berkeley, Calif: Berkeley Linguistics Society, 1991.

Talmy, Leonard. *Toward a Cognitive Semantics (vol.1): Conceptual Structure System* [M]. Cambridge, Mass.: The MIT Press, 2000a.

Talmy, Leonard. *Toward a Cognitive Semantics (vol.2): Yypology and Process in Concept Structuring* [M]. Cambridge, Mass.: The MIT Press, 2000b.

Tettamanti, M., Buccino, G., Saccuman, M. C., et al. Listening to action-related sentences activates fronto-parietal motor circuits[J]. *Journal of Cognitive Neuroscience*, 2005, 17(2): 273-281.

Whiteny, C., Huber, W., Klann, J., et al. Neural correlates of narrative shifts during auditory story comprehension[J]. *NeuroImage*, 2009, 47(1): 360-366.

Welson, R. A. & Keil, F. C. The MIT Encyclopedia of the Cognitive Sciences. Cambridge, Mass.: The MIT Press, 1999.

Van Valin, Robert D., Jr. and Randy J. Lapolla. *Syntax: Structure, Meaning, and Function*. Cambridge: Cambridge University Press, 1997.

Zhang S. Q. & Wang J. Delivery Event and Its Variants: A Cognitive-Functional Perceptive [J]. *US-China Foreign Language*, 2020, Vol. 18.

Zwaan, R. A., Taylor, L. J. Seeing, acting, understanding: motor resonance in language comprehension[J]. *Journal of Experimental Psychology: General*, 2006, 135(1): 1-11.

Oxford Advanced Learner's English-Chinese Dictionary, Seventh Edition. Oxford University Press, 2009.

Corpus of Contemporary American English (COCA): https://www.english-corpora.org/coca/

BLCU Corpus Center (BCC): https://bcc.blcu.edu.cn/lang/zh

British National Corpus: http://www.natcorp.ox.ac.uk/

官群 (Guan, Q.). 具身认知观对语言理解的新诠释–心理模拟: 语言理解的一种手段 [J]. 心理科学, 2007, 30(5): 1252-1256.

程琪龙 (Cheng, Q. L.). 逼进语言系统[M]. 南京: 东南大学出版社, 2002.

程琪龙 (Cheng, Q. L.).神经认知语言学引论[M]. 北京: 外文出版社, 2005.

程琪龙 (Cheng, Q. L.).概念框架和认知[M].上海: 上海外语教育出版社, 2006.

程琪龙, 张时倩 (Cheng & Zhang). 击撞事件及其变式. 山东外语教学, 2012, 33(4): 8.

程琪龙 (Cheng, Q. L.). "给予"认知事件框架及其识解变式[J]. 中国外语, 2019, 16 (2): 24-32.

程琪龙, 程倩雯 (Cheng & Cheng). 词汇进路和构式进路的互补研究[M]. 上海: 上海外语教育出版社, 2020.

束定芳 (Shu Dingfang). 认知语义学[M]. 上海: 上海外语教育出版社, 2008.

魏小兰 (Wei Xiaolan). 递送事件及其变式[J].当代外语研究, 2015(05):29-34.

张道真 (Zhang Daozhen). 现代英语用法词典 (*A Dictionary of Current English Usage*) [Z]. 北京: 外语教育与研究出版社, 2003.

孟琮 (Meng Zong).《汉语动词用法词典》(*A Dictionary of Chinese Verb Usage*). 商务印书馆, 1999.

章凤花 (Zhang Fenghua). 撞击事件构式的概念框架认知研究. 2008

张时倩, 王俭 (Zhang Shiqian & Wang Jian). 具身认知视域下的语言身－脑－形三维模式初探——以获取事件及其构式为例 [J]. 上海理工大学学报 (社会科学版), 2023(1): 38-44

《现代汉语词典》(*Contemporary Chinese Dictionary*) 第 7 版. 商务印书馆, 2016.

Appendix 1

Corpus of English Obtaining Verbs and Constructions

Verb	Example	Construction	Source	No.
book	I have booked <u>your passage</u>.	［名宾］	词典	1
	They have booked <u>a number of bedrooms</u> there.	［名宾］	词典	
		［原位／原属］		2
	He booked <u>me a single room</u> at my usual hotel.	［终属］（双宾）	牛津字典	3
	I've booked two tickets <u>for</u> us to see "Carmen".	［受益人］	剑桥词典	4
	She had booked three seats <u>on the plane</u>.	［地点］	词典	5
	I have booked a table <u>at the Swan</u>	［地点］	牛津字典	
		［价格／代价］		6
		［工具］		7
	We have booked two seats <u>for the theatre</u> for Friday evening.	［目的］	词典	8
	So the Hall was booked <u>for the meeting</u>.	［目的］	词典	
	How do you book a hotel <u>via</u> email?	［途径］	谷歌	9
		［职位］		13
		［具体工种］		14
buy	So he went off and bought <u>the tickets</u>	［名宾］	词典	1
	<u>Honest politicians</u> cannot be bought.	［名宾］（被动）	词典	
	Carmen bought a dress <u>from Diana</u>.	［原属］	书	2
	Carmen bought <u>Mary a dress</u>.	［终属］（双宾）	书	3
	I will buy <u>him some new clothes</u> tomorrow	［终属］（双宾）	词典	
	Carmen bought a dress <u>for Mary</u>.	［受益人］	书	4
	They had bought some forniture <u>in Stamton</u>	［地点］	词典	5
	Carmen bought a dress <u>at Bloomingdale's for $50</u>.	［地点］［价格／代价］	书	
	We bought it <u>for very little money</u>	［价格／代价］	词典	6
	They bought peace <u>with their freedom</u>.	［价格／代价］	词典	
		［工具］		7
		［目的］		8
	We buy all our software <u>by</u> mail order.	［途径］	谷歌	9
		［职位］		13
		［具体工种］		14
call	I called <u>him</u> this morning but he was out.	［名宾］	词典	1
	The King called <u>Parliament</u>.	［名宾］	词典	
	He called me <u>from New York</u>.	［原位］	词典	2
	I'll call <u>you a taxi</u>	［终属］（双宾）	牛津字典	3

	I'll call a taxi <u>for you</u>	［受益人］	牛津字典	4
		［地点］		5
		［价格／代价］		6
		［工具］		7
		［目的］		8
		［途径］		9
		［职位］		13
		［具体工种］		14
cash	The bank will cash <u>your cheque</u>	［名宾］	词典	1
	Where can I get this <u>cashed</u>?	［名宾］（被动）	词典	
	We would ask people to be especially careful when cashing cheques, particularly third party ones or from people they do not know.	［原属／原位］	牛津字典	2
		［终属］（双宾）		3
	Can you cash this cheque <u>for me</u>?	［受益人］	词典	4
	When the cheque was cashed <u>at a bank</u> it had been altered to £99.	［地点］	牛津字典	5
		［价格／代价］		6
		［工具］		7
		［目的］		8
		［途径］		9
		［职位］		13
		［具体工种］		14
catch	The early bird catched <u>the worm</u>	［名宾］	词典	1
		［原位／原属］		2
		［终属］（双宾）		3
		［受益人］		4
	The dog caught the stick <u>in</u> its mouth.	［地点／归属］	牛津字典	5
	<u>The cat</u> was caught <u>in the trap</u>.	［地点］	词典	
		［价格／代价］		6
	Catch the ball <u>with both hands</u>.	［工具］	词典	7
		［目的］		8
		［途径］		9
		［职位］		13
		［具体工种］		14
charter	The holiday-makers chartered <u>a boat</u> to go fishing.	［名宾］	词典	1
		［原位／原属］		2
		［终属］（双宾）		3
		［受益人］		4
		［地点］		5
		［价格／代价］		6
		［工具］		7
	Our school chartered three buses <u>for the trip</u>.	［目的］	词典	8
		［途径］		9
		［职位］		13

		［具体工种］		14
choose	<u>Who</u> was chosen as King?	［名宾］（被动）	词典	1
	I have chosen <u>them</u> beacause of the colours	［名宾］	词典	
	They were to choose a painful scene <u>from their childhoods</u>	［原属／原位］	数据库	2
	I've chosen <u>Luis a present.</u>	［终属］（双宾）	剑桥词典	3
	Millions of parents have been empowered to choose new schools <u>for their children.</u>	［受益人］	数据库	4
	He chose a shirt from the many <u>in</u> his wardrobe.	［地点］	剑桥词典	5
		［价格／代价］		6
		［工具］		7
	We chose a delicate floral pattern <u>for</u> our bedroom curtains.	［目的］	剑桥词典	8
	When people elect someone, they choose that person to represent them, <u>by</u> voting for them.	［途径］	谷歌	9
	We chose Mr.Dick <u>as our leader</u>	［职位］	词典	13
		［具体工种］		14
earn	He was at work and earning <u>money</u>	［名宾］	词典	1
	He earned <u>reputation</u> for honesty	［名宾］	词典	
	The contractors administering BasicsCards earn fees <u>from the U.K.</u>	［原属／原位］	数据库	2
	His achievement earned <u>him respect and admiration</u>	［终属］（双宾）	词典	3
	It is something we must earn <u>for</u> ourselves	［受益人］	数据库	4
	He went on to earn a college diploma <u>in</u> the United States	［地点］	数据库	5
		［价格／代价］		6
		［工具］		7
		［目的］		8
	He earned $3,000 a year <u>by</u> writing stories	［途径］	词典	9
		［职位］		13
		［具体工种］		14
fetch	Fetch <u>your supper</u> yourself,Robbert.	［名宾］	词典	1
	She's gone to fetch the kids <u>from school.</u>	［原属／原位］	词典	2
	I asked her to fetch <u>me an evening paper.</u>	［终属］（双宾）	词典	3
	She'd asked me to fetch water <u>for</u> her from the pump and I brought back a half-full metal bucket.	［受益人］	数据库	4
		［地点］		5
		［价格／代价］		6
		［工具］		7
		［目的］		8
		［途径］		9
		［职位］		13
		［具体工种］		14
find	She had found <u>a situation</u>	［名宾］	词典	1

	We know that the DNA that we find <u>from</u> Richard DeSalvo is the same as the DNA that we find from Albert DeSalvo	［原属／原位］	数据库	2
	Can you find <u>me a good one</u>?	［终属］（双宾）	词典	3
	I think I can find <u>you something to do.</u>	［终属］（双宾）	词典	
	Can you find my bag <u>for</u> me?	［受益人］	牛津字典	4
	He had found their address <u>in the directory</u>	［地点］	谷歌	5
	Elephants are found <u>in Africa.</u>	［地点］	牛津字典	
	He found trouble <u>with the first paragraph.</u>	［地点／具体处］	词典	
		［价格／代价］		6
	How do I find vehicle owner <u>by</u> plate number?	［工具］	谷歌	7
	Researchers are hoping to find a cure <u>for</u> the disease.	［目的］	剑桥词典	8
	Finding a way <u>through</u> the legislation is impossible without expert advice.	［途径］	谷歌	9
		［职位］		13
		［具体工种］		14
gain	He gained <u>full marks</u> in the examination.	［名宾］	词典	1
	Each of boys has gained <u>a price.</u>	［名宾］	词典	
	Mike has gained <u>a reputation</u> as an expert poker player.	［名宾］	词典	
	There is nothing to be gained by waiting.	［名宾］（被动）	词典	
	The department gained approval <u>from</u> a seven-member Records Conservation Board.	［原属／原位］	数据库	2
	Having Disney+ in your streaming repertoire will gain <u>you access</u> to all the original Disney, Star Wars, and Marvel content	［终属］（双宾）	数据库	3
		［受益人］		4
	He gained a doctorate <u>in</u> Chemical Engineering	［地点］		5
		［价格／代价］		6
		［工具］		7
	Trash talk and over-the-top antics have long been a way to gain attention <u>for</u> a big fight.	［目的］	数据库	8
	In qualifying, teams often try to gain an advantage <u>by</u> being the last car to leave the garage.	［途径］	数据库	9
		［职位］		13
		［具体工种］		14
gather	He is busy gathering <u>information</u> about birds.	［名宾］	词典	1
	The farmer gatherer <u>the corn</u> in August.	［名宾］	词典	
	The final element of the study was a set of interviews designed to gather firsthand insights <u>from</u> CTOs themselves	［原属／原位］	数据库	2
	Please gather <u>me some flowers.</u>	［终属］（双宾）	词典	3

	According to Weldon, the only plan the night of the shooting was to gather information <u>for Diana</u>.	［受益人］	数据库	4
		［地点］		5
		［价格／代价］		6
		［工具］		7
	Ann Veronica was gathering flowers <u>for the dinnner table</u>.	［目的］	词典	8
	Gather information <u>by factual investigation</u>	［途径］	谷歌	9
		［职位］		13
		［具体工种］		14
get	She got <u>much nice marks</u> in school.	［名宾］	词典	1
	Where did you get <u>those figures</u>?	［名宾］	词典	
	The first thing is to get <u>some work</u> to do.	［名宾］	词典	
	I got your card <u>from the hospital</u>.	［原属／原位］	词典	2
	Then I will go and get <u>you a chair</u>.	［终属］（双宾）	词典	3
	Will you get a ticket <u>for me</u>?	［受益人］	词典	4
	Is it hard to get a job <u>in Canada</u>?	［地点］	谷歌	5
	I managed to get all three suitcases <u>for under $200</u>.	［价格／代价］	剑桥词典	6
		［工具］		7
	Did you manage to get tickets <u>for the concert</u>?	［目的］	剑桥词典	8
	How can I get information about a vehicle's owner <u>by using the registration number of the vehicle</u>?	［途径］	谷歌	9
		［职位］		13
		［具体工种］		14
hire	Already they had hired <u>a big hall.</u>	［名宾］	词典	1
	He hired <u>a car</u> and a man to drive it.	［名宾］	词典	
	We hired a car <u>from a local firm</u>	［原属／原位］	牛津字典	2
	You will need to hire <u>yourself an accountant</u> and a lawyer.	［终属］（双宾）	牛津字典	3
	how to hire the best attorney <u>for you</u>	［受益人］	谷歌	4
	You can hire a car <u>at the airport</u>.	［地点］	谷歌	5
	How To Hire A Divorce Lawyer <u>With No Money</u>	［价格／代价］	谷歌	6
		［工具］		7
	The storekeeper hired ten girls <u>for the Christmas rush.</u>	［目的］	词典	8
		［途径］		9
	he persuaded the owner of The Village Voice to hire him <u>as</u> the editor of a new weekly.	［职位］	数据库	13
		［具体工种］		14
keep	I kept <u>it</u> all the time to remind me of you.	［名宾］	词典	1
	Please keep <u>the picture,</u>I do not want it.	［名宾］	词典	
		［原位／原属］		2

116

	I shall not keep you more than a few minutes.	［终属］（双宾）	词典	3
	I will keep a seat for you.	［受益人］	词典	4
		［地点］		5
		［价格／代价］		6
		［工具］		7
		［目的］		8
		［途径］		9
		［职位］		13
		［具体工种］		14
lease	We lease all our computer equipment.	［名宾］	牛津字典	1
	They leased the property from the Smith family.	［原属］	词典	2
	A local farmer leased them the land.	［终属］（双宾）	牛津字典	3
	He had never lived there but was paid $500 to lease it for Montalvo and his cousin.	［受益人］	数据库	4
	She planed to lease her apartment to a friend.	［受益人］	词典	
	Lansing and Friedkin were leasing a four-bedroom, 6,000-square-foot house in the Beverly Hills area, sources say.	［地点］	剑桥词典	5
	The Cider Press Company leases the machinery and buildings for $1300 a month.	［价格／代价］	剑桥词典	6
		［工具］		7
	It would work out cheaper overall to lease the computers for the project	［目的］	剑桥词典	8
	Can you lease or rent a car through Uber?	［途径］	谷歌	9
		［职位］		13
		［具体工种］		14
leave	The wound left a scar.	［名宾］	词典	1
		［原位／原属］		2
	Someone left you this note	［终属］（双宾）	牛津字典	3
	Someone left this note for you	［受益人］	牛津字典	4
	I will leave the arrangements in your hands.	［地点／归属］	词典	5
	She has left a number of book with me.	［地点／归属］	词典	
		［价格／代价］		6
		［工具］		7
		［目的］		8
		［途径］		9
		［职位］		13
		［具体工种］		14
order	He orders a glass of beer.	［名宾］	词典	1
	These boots can be ordered direct from the manufacturer.	［原属］	牛津字典	2
	I have orderd you some new clothes.	［终属］（双宾）	词典	3
	We ordered extra fries for the kids.	［受益人］	牛津字典	4
	How to Order Something on the Amazon Shopping App	［地点/具体处］	谷歌	5
		［价格／代价］		6

		［工具］		7
		［目的］		8
	How can you order pizza <u>over</u> the phone?	［途径］	谷歌	9
		［职位］		13
		［具体工种］		14
phone	I will phnoe you later and tell <u>you</u> about it.	［名宾］	词典	1
	He phoned <u>me</u> to say he could not come.	［名宾］	词典	
		［原位／原属］		2
	I will phone <u>you</u> the news.	［终属］（双宾）	词典	3
		［受益人］		4
		［地点］		5
		［价格／代价］		6
		［工具］		7
		［目的］		8
		［途径］		9
		［职位］		13
		［具体工种］		14
pick	This month is the time to pick <u>fruit</u>.	［名宾］	词典	1
	We would buy fresh fruit and pick fresh vegetables <u>from</u> a small garden in the back	［原位／原属］	牛津字典	2
	He picker <u>her</u> a rose.	［终属］（双宾）	词典	3
	If you pick some <u>for</u> yourself, be sure to pick some for someone who cannot,	［受益人］	谷歌	4
	Pick your own flowers <u>at</u> Parlee Farms	［地点］	谷歌	5
	You can visit the Mezger Family Zinnia Patch in Woodland to pick some <u>for</u> free.	［价格／代价］	谷歌	6
		［工具］		7
	Will you pick some flowers <u>for the dinner table?</u>	［目的］	词典	8
		［途径］		9
		［职位］		13
		［具体工种］		14
pluck	Please don't pluck <u>the flowers</u>	［名宾］	词典	1
	I stop to pluck a handful of red mutant roses <u>from an untended garden.</u>	［原位／原属］	数据库	2
	He plucked <u>her a rose.</u>	［终属］（双宾）	词典	3
	Nathaniel Healey would never pluck a flower <u>for</u> her.	［受益人］	数据库	4
	But where do we stand legally when we pluck a flower <u>in</u> any of the parks in Muscat?	［地点］	谷歌	5
		［价格／代价］		6
	You can pluck the salmon <u>with</u> your bare hands	［工具］	数据库	7
	What would happen if we pluck all the flowers of a plant <u>for</u> our use?	［目的］	谷歌	8
		［途径］		9
		［职位］		13
		［具体工种］		14

procure	Companies in the industry reported difficulty in procuring raw materials.	［名宾］	朗文字典	1
	He was able to procure a Rembrandt etching from the art dealer.	［原属］	词典	2
	They procured us a copy of the report.	［终属］（双宾）	牛津字典	3
	They procured a copy of the report for us.	［受益人］	牛津字典	4
	It is hard to procure water in the desert.	［地点］	词典	5
		［价格／代价］		6
		［工具］		7
	She managed to procure a ticket for the concert.	［目的］	牛津字典	8
	most teachers need to procure funding by writing grant requests	［途径］	数据库	9
		［职位］		13
	A friend procured a position in the bank for my brother.	［具体工种］［受益人］	词典	14
pull	He is not popular enough to pull many votes	［名宾］	词典	1
		［原位／原属］	牛津字典	2
		［终属］（双宾）		3
		［受益人］		4
		［地点］		5
		［价格／代价］		6
		［工具］		7
		［目的］		8
		［途径］		9
		［职位］		13
		［具体工种］		14
reach	Have you tried reaching her at home?	［名宾］		1
		［原位／原属］		2
	Please reach me the coffee pot.	［终属］（双宾）	词典	3
	Can you reach me that box?	［终属］（双宾）	词典	
		［受益人］		4
		［地点］		5
		［价格／代价］		6
		［工具］		7
		［目的］		8
		［途径］		9
		［职位］		13
		［具体工种］		14
rent	Most students rent rooms in their second year.	［名宾］	朗文字典	1
	We rent a house from Mr.Smith.	［原属］	词典	2
	She agreed to rent me the room.	［终属］（双宾）	牛津字典	3
	She agreed to rent the room to me.	［受益人］	牛津字典	4
	He rented a small house in Newtown for a year.	［地点］	词典	5
	You rented a tuxedo for two hundred dollars? Are you crazy?	［价格／代价］	朗文词典	6
		［工具］		7

	They rented a cabin for their voavtion.	［目的］	词典	8
	Rent a car for Lyft through the Lyft Express Drive program	［途径］	谷歌	9
		［职位］		13
		［具体工种］		14
reserve	Call ahead to reserve a room.	［名宾］	词典	1
	The use of this room is reserved to members of the staff.	［名宾］（被动）	词典	
		［原位／原属］		2
	I'm awfully sorry, but we've forgotten to reserve you a table.	［终属］（双宾）	剑桥词典	3
	These seats are reserved for special guests	［受益人］	牛津字典	4
	I've reserved a table at Michel's restaurant for this evening.	［地点］	词典	5
	To reserve a table for £5 call	［价格／代价］	朗文词典	6
	I reserved them by phone yesterday in the name of Tremin.	［工具］	剑桥词典	7
	Some major airports that want to reserve runway space for the airlines are discouraging corporate aviation.	［目的］	数据库	8
	reserve a room via a mobile app	［途径］	谷歌	9
		［职位］		13
		［具体工种］		14
save	So far, I've saved about £500.	［名宾］	朗文字典	1
	He saved the boy from the drowning.	［原位／原属］	词典	2
	It will save me 50p if I buy large-size box	［终属］（双宾）	词典	3
	I've save you the rooms you had.	［终属］（双宾）	词典	
	I have saved these cherries for you.	［受益人］	词典	4
		［地点］		5
		［价格／代价］		6
		［工具］		7
	He's been saving his allowance for a new bike.	［目的］	牛津字典	8
	We could save the country a whole bunch of money by doing away with Congress.	［途径］	数据库	9
		［职位］		13
		［具体工种］		14
secure	He seucured the legal rights of Hungary.	［名宾］	词典	1
	He also asked if there were any difficulties in securing the necessary funding from the Dept.	［原位／原属］	数据库	2
	He secured himself a place at law school.	［终属］（双宾）	牛津字典	3
	He secured a place for himself at law school.	［受益人］	牛津字典	4
	He secured a position in a store.	［地点］	词典	5
		［价格／代价］		6
	Nero is also accused of endangering Gray by failing to secure him in the back of a police van with a seat belt	［工具］	数据库	7

	Are you finding it harder to secure financing <u>for your work</u>?	[目的]	数据库	8
	We have secured our tickets <u>for</u> the school play.	[目的]	词典	
	The attempt to forge an alliance was implied in that AD sought to secure their backing <u>by</u> endorsing an economic policy	[途径]	数据库	9
		[职位]		13
		[具体工种]		14
shoot	Pristash could not bring himself to shoot <u>a deer</u> on a hunting trip after the war.	[名宾]	数据库	1
		[原位／原属]		2
		[终属]（双宾）		3
		[受益人]		4
	We can no longer shoot what we want <u>in</u> the woods.	[地点]	数据库	5
		[价格／代价]		6
	Slaughterhouses shoot animals in the head <u>with</u> a stun-gun	[工具]	谷歌	7
		[目的]		8
		[途径]		9
		[职位]		13
		[具体工种]		14
slaughter	I couldn't stand to watch them slaughter <u>the cattle</u>.	[名宾]	词典	1
	<u>Thousands of cattle</u> are slaughtered here every year.	[名宾]（被动）	词典	
	Nomads have to get much of their food by slaughtering animals <u>from</u> their herds.	[原位／原属]	牛津字典	2
		[终属]（双宾）		3
		[受益人]		4
		[地点]		5
		[价格／代价]		6
	How do you slaughter a cow <u>with</u> a knife?	[工具]	谷歌	7
	At present the abattoir is slaughtering animals <u>for</u> the domestic market.	[目的]	牛津字典	8
		[途径]		9
		[职位]		13
		[具体工种]		14
steal	Someone has stolen <u>my watch</u>.	[名宾]	词典	1
	A theif stole some books <u>from that shop</u>.	[原位／原属]	词典	
	<u>The idea</u> is stolen wholesale <u>from</u> the United States.	[原位／原属]	数据库	
		[终属]（双宾）		3
	You hired this guy to steal the secret code <u>for</u> yourself!	[受益者]	数据库	4

	It opens the door for Portland to steal one of the first two in Oracle.	［地点］	数据库	5
		［价格／代价］		6
	you steal a basketball off the dribble with one hand,	［工具］	谷歌	7
	They stole home-field advantage for the play-offs.	［目的］	数据库	8
	to steal victory by collaborating with despotic governments.	［途径］	数据库	9
		［职位］		13
		［具体工种］		14
vote	I always vote Labour.	［名宾］	词典	1
		［原位／原属］		2
	Parliament has voted the town a large sum of money for a new road.	［终属］（双宾）	词典	3
		［受益人］		4
		［地点］		5
		［价格／代价］		6
		［工具］		7
	Parliament has voted the town a large sum of money for a new road.	［目的］	词典	8
		［途径］		9
	The College of Cardinals voted him Pope.	［职位］	牛津字典	13
		［具体工种］		14
win	He won praises for his modesty.	［名宾］	词典	1
	Afax won the European cup from Inter Milan.	［原位／原属］	词典	
	The proposals have won enthusiastic support from the government and the media.	［原位／原属］	数据库	2
	You've won yourself a trip to New York.	［终属］（双宾）	牛津字典	3
	He soon won a reputation for himself.	［受益者］	词典	4
	He won the first palce in the competition.	［地点］	词典	5
	He won his post after years of striving.	［价格／代价］	词典	6
		［工具］		7
		［目的］		8
	a politically motivated effort to win votes by demonizing a class of citizens.	［途径］	数据库	9
		［职位］		13
		［具体工种］		14
accept	Will you accept the invitation?	［名宾］	词典	1
	Currently, lawmakers can not accept contributions from lobbyists.	［原属］	数据库	2
		［终属］（双宾）		3
	Among parents, mothers were less likely than fathers to accept a vaccine for their child.	［受益者］	数据库	4
		［地点］		5
		［价格／代价］		6

		［工具］		7
	She said she'd accept $15 for it.	［目的］	牛津字典	8
		［途径］		9
	I cannot accept you as my assistant.	［职位］	词典	13
		［具体工种］		14
accumulate	They quickly accumulated a large fortune.	［名宾］	词典	
	They set to work accumulating a huge mass of data.	［名宾］	词典	1
	to accumulate considerable capital from their commercial enterprises.	［原位／原属］	数据库	2
		［终属］（双宾）		3
		［受益人］		4
	The seed starts to accumulate a huge amount of starch in the endosperm.	［地点／具体处］	牛津字典	5
	Google and the Internet means that we can accumulate vast quantities of information with little effort.	［代价］	牛津字典	6
		［工具］		7
	The Browns accumulate draft picks for their rebuild.	［目的］	数据库	8
	By investing wisely she accumulated a fortune.	［途径］	牛津字典	9
		［职位］		13
	He accumulated a fortune in the music business.	［具体工种］	剑桥词典	14
acquire	Sophia had acquired confidence,	［名宾］	词典	
	With the money he had won he was able to acquire some property.	［名宾］	词典	1
	She had acquired information from lawyer Pratt.	［原位／原属］	词典	2
		［终属］（双宾）		3
		［受益人］		4
	By the end of his life he had acquired substantial property in Lynn	［地点］	牛津字典	5
	She acquired the painting at a jumble sale for the princely sum of 25p.	［价格／代价］	剑桥词典	6
		［工具］		7
	The team has yet to acquire the land for the stadium	［目的］	数据库	8
	The ability to use a language can be acquired by the act of using the language.	［途径］	词典	9
		［职位］		13
	Paul Getty acquired a fortune in the oil business.	［具体工种］	词典	14
appropriate	The minister was found to have appropriated a great deal of government money.	［名宾］	词典	
	You should not appropriate other people's belongings without their permission.	［名宾］	词典	1
	He often appropriates my ideas.	［名宾］	词典	

	The accompanying images were appropriated from films and video but share certain visual qualities.	［原位／原属］	牛津字典	2
		［终属］（双宾）		3
		［受益人］		4
		［地点］		5
		［价格／代价］		6
		［工具］		7
	His land was appropriated by the Army for use as a training ground.	［名宾］（被动） ［目的］	词典	8
	The council should appropriate land for a new motorway.	［目的］	词典	
		［途径］		9
		［职位］		13
		［具体工种］		14
borrow	May I borrow your bag?	［名宾］	词典	1
	Many words in English have been borrowed from French.	［原位／原属］	词典	2
	You could easily have borrowed a book from your local library.	［原属］	数据库	
		［终属］（双宾）		3
		［受益人］		4
		［地点］		5
		［价格／代价］		6
	You borrow money (with your credit card or loan)	［工具］	谷歌	7
	to borrow a car for the prom.	［目的］	数据库	8
	The government borrows this money in financial markets, by selling bonds	［途径］	谷歌	9
		［职位］		13
		［具体工种］		14
cadge	No, no, I won't even try to cadge some of her bottle.	［名宾］	数据库	1
	He would show up to cadge drinks and meals from the others.	［原属］	数据库	2
		［终属］（双宾）		3
	But first I cadged for myself two thick and hefty wood-chopping sections of beautifully grained cypress;	［受益人］	牛津字典	4
	He was cadging money on the street.	［地点］	谷歌	5
		［价格／代价］		6
	cadging money with boxes.	［工具］	谷歌	7
	You may be able to cadge a tin of warm water for shaving	［目的］	牛津字典	8

	He had cadged the production dollars <u>by</u> promising the producer a two-for-one deal that never came.	［途径］	牛津字典	9
		［职位］		13
		［具体工种］		14
collect	Their work was to collect <u>information</u> and distribute literature.	［名宾］	词典	1
	<u>Innumerable taxes</u> were collected by the warlords.	［名宾］（被动）	词典	
	He collected <u>the garbage</u> at five o'colck.	［名宾］	词典	
	The startup also began working on a tool to collect images <u>from a website called Insecam</u>	［原位／原属］	数据库	2
		［终属］（双宾）		3
	We're collecting (money) <u>for</u> the homeless.	［受益人］	剑桥词典	4
	The robot is designed to collect Garbage <u>at</u> foot path, public places	［地点］	谷歌	5
		［价格／代价］		6
		［工具］		7
	We're collecting signatures <u>for</u> a petition.	［目的］	牛津字典	8
	The CHWs were able to collect more reasonable data <u>by</u> explaining to the parents that their answers did not make sense	［途径］	数据库	9
		［职位］		13
		［具体工种］		14
exact	No doubt they will exact <u>payment</u> in due course.	［名宾］	牛津字典	1
	He exacted money <u>from a conquered man</u>.	［原属］	词典	2
		［终属］（双宾）		3
		［受益人］		4
		［地点］		5
		［价格／代价］		6
		［工具］		7
	The victors exacted ransoms <u>for their hostages</u>.	［目的］	词典	8
		［途径］		9
		［职位］		13
		［具体工种］		14
grab	The thief suddenly grabbed <u>the bag</u> and dashed off with it.	［名宾］	词典	1
	She eagerly grabbed <u>the chance</u> to travel.	［名宾］	词典	
	Jim grabbed a cake <u>from</u> the plate.	［原位／原属］	牛津字典	2
		［终属］（双宾）		3
	Could you get there early and grab some good seats <u>for us</u>?	［受益人］	剑桥词典	4
	I quickly grab a seat with Jake and Emily <u>at</u> the rear of the room.	［地点］	牛津字典	5
		［价格／代价］		6
		［工具］		7

		［目的］		8
		［途径］		9
		［职位］		13
		［具体工种］		14
inherit	The oldest son will inherit the title.	［名宾］	词典	1
	She inherited a large amount of money from her father.	［原属］	词典	2
		［终属］（双宾）		3
		［受益人］		4
		［地点］		5
		［价格／代价］		6
		［工具］		7
	But I thought Mom wanted me to inherit this great company for the family.	［目的］	数据库	8
	You can inherit their fortune through some legal trickery	［途径］	谷歌	9
		［职位］		13
		［具体工种］		14
obtain	Carmen obtained the spare part (at the hardware store).	［名宾］	书	1
	In 1849 he obtained permission to edit a daily paper.	［名宾］	词典	
	Howard had failed to obtain a scholarship.	［名宾］	词典	
	Carmen obtained the spare part from Diana.	［原属］	书	
	Leather is obtained from animals who are slaughtered for food anyway.	［原位／原属］	牛津字典	2
		［终属］（双宾）		3
	Carmen obtained a spare part for Diana.	［受益者］	书	4
	Maps and guides can be obtained at the tourist office.	［地点］	朗文词典	5
		［价格／代价］		6
		［工具］		7
	From Hookham he obtained some money for living-expenses.	［目的］	词典	8
	the results obtained through these surveys	［途径］	朗文词典	9
		［职位］		13
		［具体工种］		14
purchase	We purchased a new car.	［名宾］	词典	1
	If China buys more from the United States, it will purchase less from other countries.	［原位／原属］	数据库	2
		［终属］（双宾）		3
	The public can purchase tickets for three performers for $79.	［受益者］	数据库	4
	They've just purchased a new house in the country.	［地点］	词典	5

126

	Carmen purchased a dress at Bloomingdale's <u>for $50.</u>	[［价格／代价］	词典	6
		［工具］		7
	I purchase them <u>for a summer trip</u> in Southeast Asia	［目的］	数据库	8
	fans are encouraged to purchase postseason strips by calling 404-577-9130.	［途径］	数据库	9
		［职位］		13
		［具体工种］		14
receive	I like to receive <u>presents</u> on my birthday.	［名宾］	词典	
·	Paul received <u>an A</u> for his composition on modern drama.	［名宾］	词典	1
	The patient received <u>the best of care.</u>	［名宾］	词典	
	He received a neatly written cheque <u>from Mrs.Raeburn.</u>	［原属］	词典	2
		［终属］（双宾）		3
		［受益人］		4
	They receive treatment <u>at</u> the jail's hospital.	［地点］	数据库	5
		［价格／代价］		6
		［工具］		7
		［目的］		8
	You can sign up to receive it <u>by</u> email	［途径］	数据库	9
		［职位］		13
		［具体工种］		14
recover	We must recover <u>our losses</u> somehow,or we shall be bankrupt.	［名宾］	词典	1
	<u>The stolen jewels</u> were finally recovered.	［名宾］（被动）	词典	
	He recovered his football <u>from the neighbour's lawn.</u>	［原位／原属］	词典	2
		［终属］（双宾）		3
		［受益人］		4
	The team recovered its lead <u>in</u> the second half.	［地点/具体处］	牛津字典	5
		［价格／代价］		6
		［工具］		7
		［目的］		8
	your chances of recovering your investment <u>through</u> the SIPC	［途径］	谷歌	9
		［职位］		13
		［具体工种］		14
regain	The patient never regained <u>consciousness.</u>	［名宾］	词典	1
	<u>The island</u> was regained <u>from the French</u> during a minor war.	［原位／原属］	词典	2
	The investment bank will look to make cuts as it tries to regain support <u>from investors.</u>	［原位／原属］	数据库	
		［终属］（双宾）		3
		［受益人］		4

127

			[地点]		5
			[价格／代价]		6
			[工具]		7
		South African borrowers would also regain access to international markets for both short- and long-term capital	[目的]	数据库	8
		Napoleon III sought to regain favour with the Catholic community by treating French Protestants harshly.	[途径]	数据库	9
			[职位]		13
			[具体工种]		14
retrieve		Send two of the service robots to retrieve the cable and clamp.	[名宾]	数据库	1
		He was trying to retrieve his coin from the trolley	[原位／原属]	数据库	2
			[终属]（双宾）		3
			[受益人]		4
			[地点]		5
			[价格／代价]		6
			[工具]		7
			[目的]		8
			[途径]		9
			[职位]		13
			[具体工种]		14
seize		The cat seized the bird.	[名宾]	词典	
		Hedwig seized an opportunity to speak to him alone.	[名宾]	词典	
		The weapons found in the house were seized by the police.	[名宾]（被动）	词典	1
		They seized the land and distributed it to the peasants.	[名宾]	词典	
		She tried to seize the gun from him.	[原位／原属]	牛津字典	2
			[终属]（双宾）		3
			[受益人]		4
			[地点]		5
			[价格／代价]		6
		The hawk seized its prey with its talons.	[工具]	词典	7
			[目的]		8
			[途径]		9
			[职位]		13
			[具体工种]		14
select		Why didn't you select a nice subject?	[名宾]	词典	1
		Use " Color Brush " to select a color from the color picke	[原位／原属]	数据库	2
			[终属]（双宾）		3
		Please select a few nice apples for my mother.	[受益人]	词典	4

	Williams was originally selected <u>in</u> the second round of the 1998 NBA Draft by Chicago.'	［地点/具体处］	牛津字典	5
		［价格／代价］		6
		［工具］		7
	'Eleven of the 40 amplified samples were selected randomly <u>for</u> DNA sequence analysis.'	［目的］	牛津字典	8
	He selected that village <u>as a base of operation</u>.	［目的］	词典	
	You can print a proof sheet and select images <u>by</u> number.	［途径］	数据库	9
	They will select a career <u>as</u> an entrepreneur as they are innovative and risk taker	［职业］	数据库	13
		［具体工种］		14
snatch	The thief snatched <u>the handbag</u> and run away.	［名宾］	词典	1
	He snatched the letter <u>out of my hand</u>.	［原位／原属］	词典	
	The bully snatched the cake <u>from the smaller boy</u>.	［原属］	词典	2
	The boy was snatched <u>from his home</u> by two armed men.	［原位］	词典	
		［终属］（双宾）		3
	Dad rush out to the garden and snatch a few azaleas <u>for</u> her	［受益人］	数据库	4
	Her handbag was snatched from her by two armed men <u>in the street</u>.	［地点］	剑桥词典	5
		［价格／代价］		6
	He would snatch the garments <u>with</u> his open mouth	［工具］	数据库	7
		［目的］		8
		［途径］		9
		［职位］		13
		［具体工种］		14
barter	The loccal people bartered <u>wheats for tools</u>.	［相互：物］	词典	12
	I had to barter <u>with the</u> locals for food.	［相互：人］	朗文字典	11
change	Will you change seats <u>with me</u>?	［相互：人］	词典	11
	Where can I change <u>English money for foreign money</u>?	［相互：物］	词典	12
exchange	Gwen exchanged <u>the dress for a shirt</u>.	［相互：物］	书	12
	Gwen exchanged the dress <u>for Mary</u>.	［受益人］	书	4
	<u>John and James</u> exchanged hats.	［双主相互］	词典	10
	Mary exchanged seats <u>with Anne</u>.	［相互：人］	词典	11
	Where can I exchange <u>my dollars for pounds</u>?	［相互：物］	词典	12
substitute	She substituted <u>a fake diamond for the orignal</u>.	［相互：物］	词典	12
swap	I'll sawp <u>three of mine for one of yours</u>.	［相互：物］	词典	12
	Will you swap <u>your knife for this pen</u>?	［相互：物］	词典	12
	The boys swapped <u>baseball cards</u>.	［名宾］	词典	1
trade	They were persuaded to <u>trade information for money</u>.	［相互：物］	词典	12

129

| | The boy traded <u>his skates</u> <u>for a cricket ba</u>t. | 〔相互：物〕 | 词典 | 12 |

Note: corpuses of other verbs and constructions appeared in the book could be obtained from the author and the team.

www.ingramcontent.com/pod-product-compliance
Lightning Source LLC
Chambersburg PA
CBHW080425270326
41929CB00018B/3169